SHAPE IT! 3

WORKBOOK

Annie Cornford and Andrew Reid

CAMBRIDGE
UNIVERSITY PRESS

CAMBRIDGE
UNIVERSITY PRESS

University Printing House, Cambridge CB2 8BS, United Kingdom

One Liberty Plaza, 20th Floor, New York, NY 10006, USA

477 Williamstown Road, Port Melbourne, VIC 3207, Australia

314–321, 3rd Floor, Plot 3, Splendor Forum, Jasola District Centre, New Delhi – 110025, India

79 Anson Road, #06–04/06, Singapore 079906

José Abascal, 56 – 1°, 28003 Madrid, Spain

Avenida Paulista, 807 conjunto 2315, 01311 -915, São Paulo, Brazi

Torre de los Parques, Colonia Tlacoquemécatl del Valle, Mexico City, cp 03200, Mexico

Cambridge University Press is part of the University of Cambridge.

It furthers the University's mission by disseminating knowledge in the pursuit of education, learning and research at the highest international levels of excellence.

www.cambridge.org
Information on this title: www.cambridge.org/9781108810586

First published 2020

20 19 18 17 16 15 14 13 12 11 10 9 8 7 6 5 4 3 2 1

Printed in Great Britain by CPI Group (UK) Ltd, Croydon CR0 4YY

A catalogue record for this publication is available from the British Library

ISBN 978-1-108-81058-6 Shape It! Student's Book with Practice Extra Level 3
ISBN 978-1-108-71481-5 Own it! Student's Book with Practice Extra Level 3

Additional resources for this publication at www.cambridge.org/shapeit

CONTENTS

STARTER

WELCOME!

VOCABULARY AND READING

Technology

1 ★ Complete the sentences with the words in the box.

apps	~~devices~~	emoji
screen	social media	video chat

1 My grandparents don't have many electronic _devices_ .
2 Do your eyes get tired when you look at the computer ________________ for a long time?
3 We learn a lot about famous people by following them on ________________ .
4 Bella likes to use ________________ so she can see the person she's talking to.
5 My favorite ________________ are Snapchat and BuzzFeed.
6 It's impossible to express some emotions with a(n) ________________ .

Feelings

2 ★★ Circle the correct words.

1 Mason gets *embarrassed* / *excited* when his mom puts his baby photos on Facebook.
2 I'm getting *angry* / *excited* about tonight's party!
3 You always do well on exams, so don't be *nervous* / *bored*.
4 Carlos was *angry* / *bored* at Jill because she forgot his birthday.
5 Mandy's crying – what's she *upset* / *excited* about?
6 We're always so busy that we don't have time to get *angry* / *bored*.

3 ★★★ Write example sentences for the words.

1 embarrassed ________________
2 app ________________
3 screen ________________

A Message on an App

4 ★ Read the conversation. How are Juan and Louise spending the summer?

____

JUAN Hey! How's the filmmaking course? Are you enjoying it?
LOUISE It's great, thanks. And you? I hope you're not getting bored.
JUAN I hardly ever get bored – I love getting new ideas and dancing in front of the group.
LOUISE Don't you sometimes feel embarrassed?
JUAN Not at all! But I'm new to street dance, so I often get upset if I forget the steps. What kind of movies are you making?
LOUISE We're not making a whole movie until the end of the course. I'm so excited about that!
JUAN So, what do they teach you?
LOUISE We're learning to use different devices like video cameras and music apps.
JUAN Cool!
LOUISE After lunch, we usually write movie scripts or practice doing makeup or costumes.
JUAN They're making a short video of our final show – I'm kind of nervous about that!
LOUISE Why? You're a great dancer! Hey, maybe I can make a movie about you one day!

5 ★★★ Answer the questions.

1 How does Juan show that he is confident?
____
2 When does Juan sometimes feel unhappy?
____
3 What is Louise excited about?
____
4 What idea does Louise have for a movie?
____

GRAMMAR IN ACTION AND VOCABULARY

Simple Present and Present Continuous with Adverbs of Frequency

1 ☆ **Put the words in the correct order to make sentences.**

1 ever / upset / gets / He / hardly

He hardly ever gets upset.

2 steps / remember / I / the / don't / always

____

3 embarrassed / dance / often / Do / when / get / you / you / ?

____

4 music / the / movies / We / for / write / the / sometimes

____

5 him / His / never / teachers / angry / get / with

____

2 ☆☆ **Circle the correct words.**

1 She *'s playing* / *plays* a computer game now.
2 I *often feel* / *'m often feeling* bored at home.
3 *Does Mario sometimes send* / *Is Mario sometimes sending* you photos?
4 The course is good. I*'m having* / *have* a great time.
5 I *usually text* / *'m usually texting* my friend when I can't do my homework.

Simple Present and Present Continuous for Future

3 ☆☆ **Complete the questions with the correct form of the verbs in parentheses. Then write the answers.**

1 What time does the class start (start)? (nine)

It starts at nine.

2 When is Tom ________ (travel) to Japan? (today)

____

3 When do we ________ (get) the exam scores? (on Friday)

____

4 When are you ________ (go) to the concert? (Saturday night)

____

Music

4 ☆ **Circle nine more music words in the sound wave.**

5 ☆☆ **Match the definitions with words in Exercise 4.**

1 a loud, round instrument you play with your hands or sticks drums
2 a person who plays music and talks on the radio or at a club ________
3 music popular in Jamaica with a strong rhythm ________
4 an electric instrument similar to a guitar with low notes ________
5 popular style of music from the southern and western U.S.A. ________
6 the artist usually speaks the words in this type of music ________

6 ☆☆ **Complete the advertisement with the words in the box.**

DJ	drums	~~fan~~	heavy metal	jazz	rap

Are you a big [1] fan of music? Do you sing like a bird or is [2] ________ more your thing (fan of Drake, maybe?). Do you play a musical instrument like the guitar or [3] ________? Or perhaps you want to be a [4] ________ because you prefer to choose the songs for the party? From relaxing, [5] ________ to fast, loud [6] ________, you can learn and practice it all at MLA Music Summer Camp. Click on the link below for more information!

MORE INFO

LISTENING AND GRAMMAR IN ACTION

A Conversation

1 ☆ **Look at the photo. Where are the people?**

____

2 ☆ **Listen to the conversation. Why does Maria go to the event in Exercise 1 every year?** S.01

____

3 ☆☆ **Listen again. Are the sentences *T* (true) or *F* (false)?** S.01

1 The organizers of MusicFest sell the tickets in a lottery. T
2 Maria doesn't pay for her ticket. ___
3 She works every evening. ___
4 Maria hears and sees all the bands. ___
5 She loves the music but doesn't like the hot weather. ___

4 ☆☆☆ **Listen again. Why do Maria and Nick mention these words?** S.01

1 excited Nick says Maria looks excited.
2 upset ______________________________
3 fans ______________________________
4 reggae singers ______________________________

Simple Past

5 ☆ **Complete the sentences with the simple past form of the verbs in parentheses.**

1 Ela wrote (write) a great song and ________ (sing) it for us last night.
2 We ________ (take) the dogs and ________ (go) for a long walk on the beach.
3 I ________ (know) you were here because I ________ (see) your coat.
4 ________ she ________ (make) a playlist for Luca's birthday party?
5 Marcus ________ (not tell) us that he ________ (have) concert tickets for all of us.

6 ☆☆ **Complete the sentences with the correct simple past form of the verbs in the box.**

be (x2)	fall	learn	not enjoy	~~play~~	work

1 The heavy metal band played really loud music.
2 We ________ the words to all the new songs.
3 They ________ very hard on their projects.
4 Joe ________ embarrassed when he ________ on the ice.
5 I ________ the concert. It ________ boring.

7 ☆☆☆ **Write questions about Maria and MusicFest. Then write the correct answers from the audio in Exercise 2.**

1 the organizers of MusicFest / send Maria a letter / ?
Did the organizers of MusicFest send Maria a letter?
No, they didn't. They sent her an email.
2 Maria / ask the organizers for a free ticket / ?
____
3 Maria / get a ticket in the lottery / ?
____
4 Maria / work in the evening last year / ?
____
5 it / rain all weekend at MusicFest last year / ?
____

WRITING

A Review of an App

1 ★ **Look at the advertisement. What do you think the app does?** ____________

2 ★★ **Read Enzo's review and check your answer to Exercise 1.**

1 WordFind is a great app for English language learners, especially when you are studying alone. Our teacher told us about it in class. He said he uses it all the time, so I decided to try it. Last week, I downloaded it on my phone, and I love it!

2 It's good because the definitions are very easy to understand. It tells you what each word means in simple English and how and when you can use it. You can also search for a word by saying it. I can't always find words when I don't know how to spell them, so this is very useful.

3 In my opinion, there are a couple of problems with it. It tells you where each word comes from and when people first used it, but I'm not interested in the history of words. Also, it's expensive – there are a lot of free dictionary apps, though maybe they're not as good.

4 Overall, I think WordFind is a great app because you can use it anywhere and it's easy to use. I would definitely recommend it.

3 ★★ **Which paragraph (1–4) …**

a explains the bad things about the app? _3_
b gives Enzo's general opinion? ___
c introduces the app? ___
d explains the good things about the app? ___

4 ★★ **Complete the *Useful Language* phrases with the words in the box.**

great ~~language~~ opinion Overall problems recommend

1 WordFind is a _language_-learning app.
2 It's __________ because you can use it anywhere.
3 I would definitely __________ it to all English language learners.
4 __________, I think it's a great app.
5 In my __________, there are a couple of __________ with it.

PLAN

5 ★★ **Write your own review. Choose a language-learning app you use and take notes.**

What is it? ____________
____
What's good about it? ____________
____
What isn't good about it? ____________
____
What's your general opinion? ____________
____
____

6 **Decide what information to include in each paragraph. Use the information in Exercise 3 to help you.**

WRITE

7 ★★★ **Write your review. Remember to include four paragraphs, the simple present and present continuous, adverbs of frequency, and phrases from the *Useful Language* box (see Student's Book, p9).**

CHECK

8 **Do you …**

- introduce the app in the first paragraph?
- write about good and bad things?
- give your general opinion?

1 What inspires you?

VOCABULARY
Describing People

1 ★ **Find 11 more personality adjectives in the word search.**

A	M	C	O	N	F	I	D	E	N	T	R
M	S	A	F	D	A	S	E	G	R	E	G
B	S	L	F	E	Y	C	U	Z	J	X	I
I	E	M	I	D	T	N	V	K	C	S	N
T	P	R	O	F	E	N	T	U	H	O	S
I	A	O	B	A	E	D	C	N	E	C	P
O	T	R	S	C	S	S	E	D	E	I	I
U	I	A	C	T	O	N	F	F	R	A	R
S	E	N	S	I	T	I	V	E	F	B	I
G	N	B	E	V	R	Y	W	B	U	L	N
F	T	R	S	E	N	S	I	B	L	E	G
N	G	H	E	L	P	F	U	L	J	W	B
T	A	L	E	N	T	E	D	B	N	Y	S

2 ★★ **Complete the sentences with words in Exercise 1.**

1 People think I'm confident, but I'm usually shy.
2 Paul isn't very ________. He likes being alone.
3 He's usually very ________. He's always smiling.
4 Kim and her brother are very different. He's silly and immature, but she's ________.
5 It's better to be ________ and not panic in dangerous situations.
6 I'm very ________ – I get upset easily.

3 ★★ **Complete the chart with the opposites of some of the words in Exercise 1.**

in-	1 sensitive	im-	7 ________
un-	2 ________ 3 ________ 4 ________ 5 ________ 6 ________		

4 ★★ **Complete the sentences with the opposites in the box.**

~~anxious~~ grumpy lazy shy silly

1 Martin isn't calm today. He's anxious because of his exam tomorrow.
2 I don't think I'm confident. I'm usually really ________.
3 My mother is always ________. She's not cheerful at all.
4 You're so ________ sometimes. Why can't you be more sensible?
5 When she was young, my cat was always active. Now she's just ________.

5 ★★ **Circle the correct adjectives.**

HOME ABOUT ME ARCHIVE FOLLOW

My sister, Alicia, is a very [1]*confident / talented* person because she's always sure of herself and knows what she's good at. In fact, she's pretty [2]*active / ambitious* – she has a lot of goals and things she wants to achieve. She's also smart and really [3]*patient / talented* – she can play the piano and is very good at sports. The only "problem" is that she's not very [4]*cheerful / sociable* – she doesn't like going to parties and she doesn't have many friends. But if I have a problem, she's always [5]*helpful / calm* and tries to solve it. Alicia is [6]*sensitive / patient*, too – she doesn't get angry, even when other people make really big mistakes. My sister is my hero!

Explore It!

Guess the correct answer.

Scientists believe that people who are … live longer than average.

a cheerful b confident c grumpy

Find another interesting idea about how to live longer. Write a question and send it to a classmate in an email, or ask them in the next class.

READING

An Article

1 ☆ Read the article quickly and answer the questions.

1 What is the name of the young man in photo A?

____

2 What is the name of the wave in photo B?

____

2 ☆☆ Match the words in bold in the article with the definitions.

1 very surprised *amazed*
2 a physical or mental power to do something ______
3 a person who teaches other people ______
4 water that moves over the top of the ocean ______
5 very difficult ______
6 wanting to do something very much ______

3 ☆☆ Are the sentences *T* (true) or *F* (false)? Correct the false sentences.

1 Derek's favorite surfer was also named Derek. *F*
Derek's father's favorite surfer was also named Derek.
2 Derek didn't surf until he was a teenager. ___
____
3 Derek's father taught Derek to surf. ___
____
4 Derek can hear which direction he needs to surf in. ___
____
5 People who saw Derek in Hawaii were very surprised. ___
____
6 Derek went to Hawaii to make a movie with a producer. ___
____

4 ☆☆☆ Answer the questions in your own words.

1 Why do you think Derek was determined to try surfing?
____
2 What do you think inspired the movie producer to make a movie about Derek?
____

Home Posts Archives

SURFING WITHOUT LIMITS

Derek Rabelo was born in Brazil in 1992. His father named him Derek after a famous surfing champion, Derek Ho – his father's favorite surfer. Derek's father wanted Derek to become a surfer, too, but this was going to be difficult because Derek was born blind. His father's dream to see his son surf seemed impossible!

When Derek was 17, his father told him about his dream. From that moment, Derek was **determined** to become a surfer. He went to the beach with his father every day and started taking surfing lessons with an **instructor**. Derek kept trying, and finally, he learned to surf!

Derek explains that although he can't see, he understands the noises that the **waves** make and he can hear them when they are coming. He says every part of a wave makes a different noise, so he knows which direction to surf in.

In 2012, he flew to Hawaii to surf the famous Banzai Pipeline – one of the most **challenging** and dangerous waves in the world. Local surfers were **amazed** to see the confident young blind man surf the huge wave with no problem at all.

While Derek was surfing in Hawaii, he met a movie producer who believed that Derek had an amazing **ability**. The producer decided to make a movie about him. *Beyond Sight* tells Derek's inspirational story and teaches us that nothing is impossible if you believe in yourself!

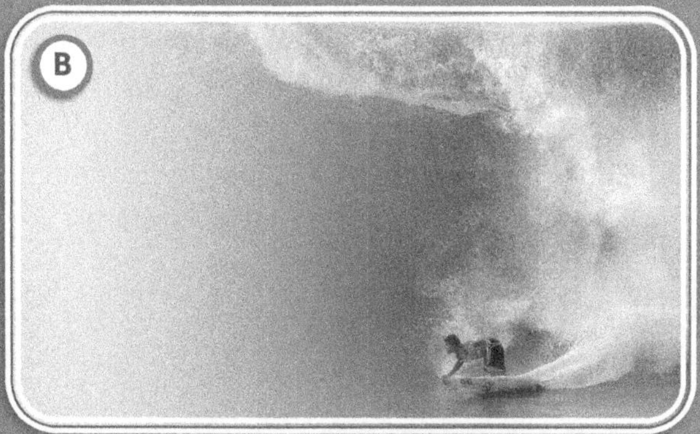

GRAMMAR IN ACTION

Simple Past and Past Continuous with *When* and *While*

1 ★ Complete the sentences with the past continuous form of the verbs in the box.

do	look	not watch
rain	~~sleep~~	work

1 I _was sleeping_ at eleven o'clock last night. That's why I didn't check my emails.

2 It ________ yesterday, so I didn't go out.

3 My mom ________ late at the office and missed dinner.

4 I ________ for clothes online, but I didn't see anything I liked.

5 What ________ you ________ in the kitchen? I heard a strange noise.

6 She ________ videos on the computer – she was studying!

2 ★★ Complete the conversation with the simple past form of the verbs in parentheses.

EMMA Hey, Ben! [1] _Did you have_ (you / have) a nice vacation?

BEN Hmm, not bad. I [2] ________ (help) my uncle in his store.

EMMA Why [3] ________ (you / do) that?

BEN Because my aunt [4] ________ (be) sick, and my uncle [5] ________ (not have) time to go to the store every day.

EMMA Wow! That's really kind of you. [6] ________ (it / be) difficult?

BEN Yeah. But my uncle [7] ________ (give) me some money for it, so I [8] ________ (buy) some new clothes.

EMMA Cool!

3 ★★ Write sentences with the simple past and past continuous and the words in parentheses.

1 I / sleep / you / call / me last night (when)
I was sleeping when you called me last night.

2 he / finish / his book / he / wait / for the bus (while)
____

3 we / live / in New York, / we / go / to a lot of museums (while)
____

4 she / not see / the puddle / she / cross / the street (when)
____

5 I / not cry / I / watch / that inspirational movie (while)
____

6 they / say / goodbye / they / leave / the party (when)
____

4 ★★ (Circle) the correct options.

One day, my wife was sick, so I [1](*drove*) / *was driving* to the drugstore to get some medicine. While I [2]*walked* / *was walking* back to the car, I noticed that I [3]*didn't have* / *wasn't having* my keys. They were still in the car with my phone! I [4]*kicked* / *was kicking* the wheels of my car when a teenager [5]*was arriving* / *arrived* on his bike and [6]*asked* / *was asking* what was wrong. I told him the story and [7]*explained* / *was explaining* that we had another car key at home, but it was five kilometers away. The boy said, "I'll get the keys" and then [8]*gave* / *was giving* me his phone to call my wife to explain what was happening. After 30 minutes, he [9]*came* / *was coming* back with the keys. While I [10]*opened* / *was opening* my car, he rode away – before I could thank him!

5 ★★★ Write a short paragraph in your notebook about a time when someone helped you or you helped someone. Use the simple past and past continuous.

VOCABULARY AND LISTENING

Phrasal Verbs

1 ☆ Circle the correct options.

1 If you have a good relationship with someone, you *get along with* / *hang out with* them.

2 When you supervise or care for someone who is old, sick, or very young, you *cheer up* / *take care of* them.

3 When you spend time with friends, you *hang out* / *deal* with them.

4 When you try to solve a problem, you *deal with* / *depend on* it.

5 If you respect and admire someone, you *look up to* / *give up* them.

6 When you make someone feel happier, you *cheer them up* / *hang them out*.

7 When you stop trying to do something because it is too difficult, you *cheer up* / *give up*.

8 When you need someone's help and support, you *look up to* / *depend on* them.

2 ☆☆ Complete the sentences with the phrasal verbs in Exercise 1.

1 I can't go out tonight. I have a lot of problems that I need to *deal with*.

2 I sometimes __________ my little brother when my parents are not at home.

3 I can't do this homework – it's too difficult. I __________!

4 I really __________ my mother. I think she's an amazing woman, and I'd like to be just like her when I'm older.

5 I __________ my sister for help and advice. I often don't know what to do without her.

6 My grandfather is feeling sad these days, so I'm trying to __________ him __________.

7 I usually __________ with friends at the park or in a café.

8 Paula doesn't __________ Susana very well. They're very different people.

A Conversation

1.01 3 ☆ Listen to the conversation. Why is Gabriel going to a concert?

a It's a family member's birthday.

b He wants to help people.

c It's his weekend job.

1.01 4 ☆☆ Listen again. Complete the notes with key words and information.

Concert
- Takes place at 1 *the park*
- Brandon's 2 __________ was sick in the past
- Concert to make money for people with same illness
- Brandon wants to make a minimum of 3 $__________ for charity.

Charity Work
- Brandon made more than 4 $__________ last month for charity.
- Jobs he did: washed 5 __________, cut grass in yards, took trash away
- Worked some afternoons and every 6 __________

5 ☆☆☆ Gabriel mentions running a race, giving up chocolate, and cutting off his hair for charity. Think of three other ways to raise money.

1 __________

2 __________

3 __________

GRAMMAR IN ACTION

Used To

1 ★ Match sentences 1–6 with a–f.

1 I used to live in the country. c
2 I didn't use to like coffee. ☐
3 I used to be really shy. ☐
4 I used to like going to the gym. ☐
5 I used to eat a lot of fast food. ☐
6 I didn't use to have many friends. ☐

a Now I don't have time.
b Now I think it's unhealthy.
c I live in a city now.
d Now I have a lot of them.
e I'm much more confident these days.
f Now I have a cup every morning.

2 ★ Complete the text with *used to* or *didn't use to*.

When I was very young, I [1] used to want to be a swimming teacher because I loved swimming and I [2] ______ like our gym teacher. Sometimes, I [3] ______ want to be an astronaut, as well, because I really liked space. When I got older, I started to get interested in computers. We [4] ______ have a good computer at home, just a very old one, but then my dad decided to buy a really good one. My parents [5] ______ let me spend much time on the computer – just a few hours a week. When I was 13, I started learning how to write my own games. I [6] ______ know how to do that before, but I had a great teacher at school who showed me how. In the future, I'd like to be a game developer!

3 ★★ Look at the photos. Complete the sentences with the correct form of *used to*.

1 I didn't use to like ice cream, but now I love it!
2 I ______, but I play tennis now.
3 I ______, but now I want to be a teacher.
4 I ______, but I have one now.
5 I ______. Now I have a new one.

4 ★★ Put the words in the correct order to make questions with *used to*.

1 you / use / to / Did / cell phones / have / ?
Did you use to have cell phones?
2 did / How / communicate / with / people / use / to / you / ?
______
3 free / in / your / What / you / did / use / do / to / time / ?
______
4 old / use / people / What / you / think / did / of / to / ?
______

5 ★★ Complete the answers to the questions in Exercise 4. Use the correct form of *used to* and the verbs in the box.

be	do	~~have~~	read	send	think (x2)	use

1 Twenty years ago, I didn't use to have a cell phone. We ______ the home phone to make calls.
2 We ______ letters and meet up a lot. Life ______ calmer then.
3 I watched TV. I ______ a lot of books, too. A lot of people now go shopping. We ______ that because we didn't have the money.
4 Good question! I ______ about them at all! I ______ I couldn't get old. I still don't think I'm old!

WRITING

A Letter to a Magazine

1 ☆ **Read the competition details. What will the writer win for the best entry?** ____________

____

Competition! Write and tell us about a helpful person in your life who you think deserves an award. As always, the winning letter appears online in next month's edition and the writer receives $100! The person you write about will also win a special award. Answer the following questions.

- Who is the most helpful person you know?
- What do/did they do to help you?
- Why do you think they deserve to win an award?

2 ☆ **Read the letter to a magazine. Does the writer answer the questions in Exercise 1 in the same order?** ____________

The most helpful person I know is my English teacher, Mrs. Davies. In my [1] opinion, she should definitely win an award. Here's why.

A few years ago, I used to go to a different school, and I liked it very much. Then my parents got new jobs in a different city, and I changed schools. In the new school, I was shy and not at all confident. I didn't make any new friends. The only person who really noticed this was Mrs. Davies. She helped me by talking to me in class and putting me in groups with other friendly students. She also often asked questions that she knew I could answer in front of the class. [2] ____________ me, that was a very kind thing to do. [3] ____________, I think I became more confident and sociable because of Mrs. Davies!

In my [4] ____________, Mrs. Davies deserves an award because she's the calmest and most patient teacher at our school. She's also sensitive to people's feelings and always wants to help her students. She helped me through a difficult situation, and she also inspired me to like English!

3 ☆☆ **Complete the *Useful Language* phrases in the letter with the words in the box.**

~~opinion~~	personally	to	view

4 ☆☆ **Read the letter again. Are the sentences *T* (true) or *F* (false)?**

1 The writer wasn't very happy at her old school. F

2 She went to a new school because her parents wanted to live in the country. ____

3 Her teacher asked her easy questions in class to help her. ____

4 The writer thinks Mrs. Davies should win the award because she helped build her confidence. ____

PLAN

5 ☆☆ **Write your own letter to a magazine. Think of a helpful person you know. What do/did they do to help you? Why should they win an award?**

WRITE

6 ☆☆☆ **Write your letter. Remember to include three paragraphs, past tenses, *used to*, and phrases from the *Useful Language* box (see Student's Book, p17).**

CHECK

7 **Do you ...**

- introduce the person in the first paragraph?
- say why the person should win an award?
- use language for giving opinions?

1 REVIEW

VOCABULARY

1 Match the people with the adjectives in the box.

active ambitious calm cheerful
confident helpful inspiring patient
sensible sensitive sociable talented

1 She runs every morning and goes to the gym on the weekend, too! ______________
2 Mark always wants to do things for other people. ______________
3 He never gets nervous. He always looks relaxed. ______________
4 Sara can play the piano very well. She's also an amazing singer. ______________
5 Paula loves talking to people and making new friends. ______________
6 John is 100 percent sure about everything he does – he believes he can do anything. ______________
7 I was 45 minutes late, but Alex didn't get angry at all! ______________
8 We all look up to George. He's an amazing person. ______________
9 Kerry is always playing tennis. She wants to be a professional player one day. ______________
10 Linda is always smiling, even when everyone else is sad or tired. ______________
11 Be careful what you say to Hannah. She gets upset very easily. ______________
12 Johann is a serious person. He always says and does the right thing. ______________

2 Circle the correct prepositions.

1 I always looked up *with* / *to* my older brother when I was young.
2 Don't look so sad. Cheer *to* / *up*!
3 I might go out today. It depends *on* / *of* the weather.
4 I tried running five kilometers yesterday, but I was tired and gave *up* / *out* after four kilometers.
5 You need to be very patient to deal *with* / *on* little children.
6 Everyone gets *in* / *along* with Eduardo because he's really cheerful and sociable.
7 I was hanging *out* / *on* with my friends last night.
8 I used to take care *with* / *of* my little sister when she was a baby.

GRAMMAR IN ACTION

3 Complete the sentences with the simple past and past continuous form of the verbs in parentheses.

1 I ______________ (walk) to the store when it ______________ (start) to rain.
2 My friend ______________ (call) me while I ______________ (write) him a text.
3 What ________ Harry and Abby ________ (do) when they ______________ (hear) the news?
4 He ______________ (find) an expensive ring when he ______________ (clean) their house.
5 We ______________ (leave) Tom's house when Lisa ______________ (arrive).
6 While I ______________ (cross) the street, my phone ______________ (fall) out of my pocket.

4 **Complete the conversation with the correct form of *used to* and the verbs in parentheses.**

A How old is your brother now?

B He's nine.

A Wow! I remember when he was a little baby. He [1] ________________ (be) so sweet!

B Yes. And I [2] ________________ (take) care of him, too! I [3] ________________ (read) him bedtime stories!

A [4] ________________ (you / give) him food and put him to bed?

B No, I [5] ________________ (not do) that. My parents [6] ________________ (do) it. He's changed a lot. He really [7] ________________ (look up) to me, but now he doesn't!

CUMULATIVE GRAMMAR

5 **Complete the text with the missing words. Circle the correct options.**

When my mother was younger, she [1] _____ a singer. I [2] _____ this until recently! She [3] _____ short, blond hair, and she [4] _____ really strange clothes. In her first year at college, she [5] _____ some other people who wanted to form a band. The other people quickly [6] _____ out that she was a really talented singer, so they asked her to join in. She [7] _____ famous or anything like that, but she had a lot of fun. Unfortunately, I [8] _____ any recordings of her singing. They [9] _____ smartphones or video cameras then, so I can't see what she looked like. It's difficult to believe that my mom used to be a singer because she [10] _____ very serious and sensible these days! She has long, dark hair and she [11] _____ in a bank! Where did that young pop singer [12] _____?

1	a is	b was being	c was
2	a not know	b didn't knew	c didn't know
3	a was having	b did have	c used to have
4	a wore	b was wearing	c wear
5	a was meeting	b met	c meets
6	a found	b find	c were finding
7	a weren't	b wasn't being	c didn't use to be
8	a don't have	b have not	c doesn't have
9	a weren't having	b didn't used to have	c didn't use to have
10	a always	b is always	c always is
11	a works	b usually works	c work
12	a goes	b went	c go

2 What is art?

VOCABULARY

Visual and Performing Arts

1 ☆ **Complete the visual and performing arts words. Then match the words with photos a–h.**

1 filmmaking [d]
2 s__ __ee__ __ a__t [ ]
3 __o__ __e__ __o__a__y __a__ __e [ ]
4 __a__ __io__ __e__i__n [ ]
5 s__u__p__u__e [ ]
6 p__o__o__ __a__h__ [ ]
7 a__c__i__e__ __u__e [ ]
8 il__u__t__a__io__ [ ]

a

b
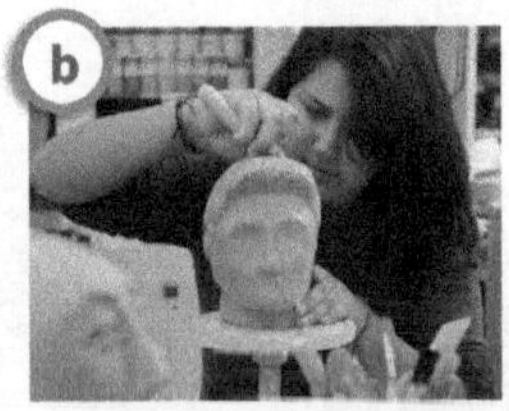
c

d

e

f
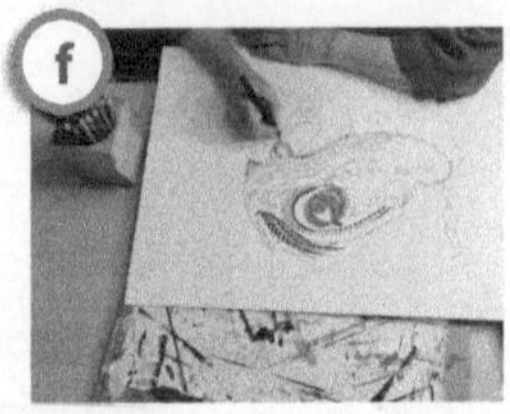
g

h

2 ☆☆ **Correct the sentences by changing the underlined words.**

1 You see paintings and other art forms in a performance. ______________

2 Musical theater is an inside or outside event where you can see paintings and other art forms. ______________

3 An exhibition is the action of entertaining people by dancing, singing, acting, or playing music. ______________

4 A gallery is a play in which singing and dancing tell part of the story. ______________

3 ☆☆ **Match the beginnings of the words with the ends to make the names of the people who do an activity.**

danc – illustrat – art – sculpt – filmmak – fashion design

-or -er -ist

4 ☆☆ **Match the people or things (1–6) with the definitions (a–f).**

1 contemporary dance [e]
2 fashion design [ ]
3 street art [ ]
4 filmmaker [ ]
5 sculpture [ ]
6 illustrator [ ]

a making objects that represent things, people, or ideas
b someone who draws pictures for books
c someone who creates movies for TV or theaters
d working with clothes, shoes, and sometimes hairstyles
e moving to music in a modern style
f paintings, graffiti, etc., outside in urban areas

Explore It!

Guess the correct answer.

Every … minutes, people around the world take more photos than the whole of humanity took in the 1800s.

a 2 b 10 c 45

Find another interesting fact about an art form. Write a question and send it to a classmate in an email, or ask them in the next class.

READING

A Magazine Article

1 ☆ **Look at the photo. What art form can you see and where do you think it is?**

____

2 ☆ **Read the article from an art magazine and check your answer to Exercise 1.**

3 ☆☆ **Match the words in bold in the article with the definitions.**

1 going underwater sinking
2 people who work to protect the environment ______________
3 an orange-brown metal ______________
4 put something into position ______________
5 an ability to achieve something ______________
6 keep or maintain something in its position ______________

4 ☆☆ **Read the article again. Answer the questions.**

1 Where did Lorenzo Quinn study art?
He studied art in the U.S.A.
2 What are Quinn's sculptures normally made from?
____
3 Which important problem does *Support* deal with?
____
4 How are the giant hands "helping" the Ca' Sagredo Hotel?
____
5 How did Quinn's family help with *Support*?
____
6 Who can do something about climate change, according to Quinn?
____

5 ☆☆☆ **Answer the questions in your own words.**

1 What's your favorite form of art? Why do you like it?
____
____
2 What other important issues does art often deal with? Think of two examples.
____
____

Support: An Art Installation

Sculptor Lorenzo Quinn is the first artist to **install** a work of art directly into the Grand Canal in Venice. But who is he, and what does his work of art mean?

Quinn was born in Rome, but he has lived in Spain and in the U.S.A., where he studied art. He hasn't always been a sculptor. He has also been a singer, and he has acted in movies – once as the painter Salvador Dalí!

His sculptures have appeared at exhibitions internationally. He usually works with metals such as **bronze**, steel, and aluminum. But what inspired him to make visual art with two enormous hands?

Together with many scientists and **conservationists**, Quinn believes that the Mediterranean Sea has risen and is still rising because of climate change. Because of higher water levels in the Grand Canal, the historic city of Venice is slowly **sinking**.

The art installation, called *Support*, which Quinn created for the Venice Art Biennale exhibition, warns us about the danger of rising water levels in this amazing city. The two giant hands **"hold up"** the famous Ca' Sagredo Hotel on Venice's Grand Canal.

Quinn used his son's hands as models for the huge sculptures to show the **potential** of the next generation. The message is that the future is in their hands.

GRAMMAR IN ACTION

Present Perfect with Regular and Irregular Verbs

1 ☆ **Circle the correct options.**

1 He has *use* / *used* bronze to make the sculpture.
2 *Have* / *Has* you watched that video about Dalí?
3 They haven't *visit* / *visited* many exhibitions.
4 I have never *meet* / *met* a street artist.
5 *Has* / *Have* your art teacher taught you how to use spray paint?
6 A Have they visited the new gallery?
B Yes, they *have* / *haven't*.

2 ☆ **Complete the sentences with the present perfect form of the verbs in parentheses.**

1 We _have been_ (be) to a very interesting exhibition.
2 She ________ (not do) any contemporary dance.
3 The children ________ (make) some plastic models.
4 I ________ (see) some beautiful artwork today.
5 ________ you ________ (take) photography classes?
6 Sofia's mom ________ (write) to her art teacher.

3 ☆☆ **Complete the sentences with the present perfect form of the verbs in the box.**

be	draw	~~have~~	make	not see	not write

1 The art installation _has had_ an enormous number of visitors.
2 We ________ the new exhibition yet.
3 ________ Lorenzo Quinn ________ any new sculptures this year?
4 My favorite singer ________ many good songs this year.
5 ________ you ever ________ a picture of a rabbit? It isn't easy!
6 I ________ never ________ on a gondola on the Grand Canal. Have you?

4 ☆☆ **Complete the sentences with *been* or *gone*.**

1 I've _been_ to the art store. Look what I bought.
2 Helena's ________ into town, but she's normally back home by five o'clock.
3 My parents have ________ to Venice many times.
4 We've ________ to see the exhibition and we loved it.
5 He's ________ to the gallery. He's meeting the artist.

5 ☆☆ **Complete the text with the present perfect form of the verbs in the box.**

change	ever take	~~join~~	make	train

JOIN OUR SALSA DANCE CLASSES!

Read what some of our students wrote about it:

"My friends and I [1] _have joined_ many different classes, but the salsa class is the best – it's awesome!"

"This is the best class I [2] ________. Everyone is so welcoming. I [3] ________ some great new friends."

"Salsa dancing [4] ________ my life! My teacher [5] ________ in Colombia and the Caribbean, and her classes are fun and very exciting!"

6 ☆☆☆ **Write questions and answers.**

1 your brother / ever read / *Death in Venice* / ?
No / see / the movie
Has your brother ever read Death in Venice?
No, he hasn't, but he has seen the movie.

2 they / ever visit / Rio / ?
No / be / to São Paulo
____
____

3 she / ever win / first prize in a competition / ?
No / come in second
____
____

4 you / ever make / a video / ?
No / take / some great photos on my phone
____
____

VOCABULARY AND LISTENING

Music and Theater

1 Match the beginnings of the sentences (1–6) with the ends (a–f).

1 The words of a song [f]
2 A recording studio is where [ ]
3 The words an actor says [ ]
4 The audience is the people [ ]
5 You have an audition when [ ]
6 During a rehearsal [ ]

a are called the lines.
b you practice a play, concert, or show.
c who are listening to the orchestra.
d singers and musicians record their music.
e you want a part or role in a play or show.
f are called the lyrics.

2 Circle the correct options.

1 When the *orchestra* / *audience* stopped playing their instruments, we stood up and clapped.
2 In the final *show* / *scene*, the friends say goodbye and the movie ends.
3 I really want the *line* / *part* of Romeo in the school production of Shakespeare's *Romeo and Juliet*.
4 What's your favorite type of *part* / *show*: dance, music, or theater?

3 Answer the questions.

1 Have you ever written lyrics for a song? What was the song about?

____

____

2 Have you ever performed in a play or a show? What part did you have?

____

____

3 Have you ever played in or been to see an orchestra? Which one?

____

____

A Conversation

4 2.01 **Listen to Melanie and David talking about Alma Deutscher, a young musician. Answer the questions.**

1 How does Melanie feel about Alma at the beginning of the conversation?

____

2 Does she feel differently at the end?

____

5 2.01 **Listen again and answer the questions.**

1 How does David know so much about Alma Deutscher?
He watched a show about her on YouTube.
2 What art form is Alma's *Cinderella*?

____

3 What musical instruments does Alma play?

____

4 Where was the performance of *Cinderella*?

____

5 How does Alma get some of her ideas and melodies?

____

6 What activity is a waste of time, according to Alma?

____

6 Find out about another talented young person like Alma Deutscher. Write a short paragraph about their life and achievements in your notebook.

GRAMMAR IN ACTION

Present Perfect with *Already, Just, Still,* and *Yet*

1 ★ Match sentences 1–6 with a–f.

1 My mom's just found her glasses. [c]
2 I haven't seen that movie yet. [ ]
3 The show has already started. [ ]
4 She still hasn't heard from Joel. [ ]
5 I've just had a second audition. [ ]
6 The children haven't gone to bed yet. [ ]

a She hopes he calls soon.
b I hope I get the part.
c Now she can see the stage.
d They'll be tired in the morning.
e We've missed the beginning.
f We have tickets to see it tomorrow.

2 ★★ Look at the photos. Write sentences about what has just happened.

1 she / cut his hair
She has just cut his hair.
2 The children / finish school for the day
______
3 they / go swimming
______
4 he / make a cake
______
5 the girls / see a funny movie
______
6 the girl / give her some flowers
______

3 ★★ Circle the letter of the correct sentence.

1 (a) I've already seen the art exhibition.
  b Already I've seen the art exhibition.
2 a Dylan just has left for school.
  b Dylan has just left for school.
3 a She hasn't cleaned up her room still!
  b She still hasn't cleaned up her room!
4 a Have you bought the orchestra tickets yet?
  b Have you bought yet the orchestra tickets?
5 a Liz and Eva have come back from the movies just.
  b Liz and Eva have just come back from the movies.

4 ★★ Rewrite the sentences putting the words in parentheses in the correct position.

1 The gallery has announced an exciting event. (just)
The gallery has just announced an exciting event.
2 Have you heard about the Picasso exhibition? (yet)
______
3 Someone has discovered an unknown painting. (just)
______
4 The gallery has bought it from a collector in Paris. (just) ______
5 It seems they have agreed on a fair price. (already)
______
6 They haven't told anyone how much they paid, though. (still) ______

5 ★★★ Put the words in the correct order.

1 you / yet / seen / new / the / Shrek movie / Have / ?
Have you seen the new Shrek movie yet?
2 art gallery / already / to / Enzo / the / has / gone / .
______
3 still / art project / finished / Susie / her / hasn't / .
______
4 audition / you / your / had / yet / Have / ?
______
5 have / They / in town / just / held / an exhibition / .
______
6 three times / been / have / We / to / already / the theater / this month / !
______

WRITING

A Review

1 ☆ **Look at the photo. Circle the correct answer.**

The New Dance School is …

a a classical orchestra.
b a music group.
c a group of dancers.

2 ☆ **Read the review. Why does the reviewer recommend The New Dance School?**

___

___

1 Have you seen The New Dance School yet? I've never heard anything like it before. The band is perfect for lovers of international music – it's the best performance I've ever been to!

2 The New Dance School's music isn't exactly rock. It's a bit like world music, but you can really dance to it! The musicians are all really talented. They create powerful rhythms with a number of different instruments, like sitars, bongos, and steel drums – it's amazing.

3 What I liked about it was that the performers were so happy and there was a lot of movement in their music. They make you feel cheerful. I was sitting in the audience, but I really wanted to get up and dance!

4 I saw them at my local community center. It was so cool! These musicians haven't been together very long, but they have a big future! The New Dance School is playing at the Newport Music Festival, so don't miss it. I recommend it because the music has great energy and it makes you want to dance.

3 ☆ **Which paragraph (1–4) …**

a gives a description of the band and its music? 2
b explains what the reviewer liked / didn't like about it? ___
c gives details of where you can see the band? ___
d explains who the band's audience is? ___

4 ☆ **Circle the correct words in the *Useful Language* phrases. Then check in the review.**

1 I've *never* / *ever* heard anything like it before.
2 It's *play* / *playing* at …
3 I *recommend* / *recommending* it because …
4 It's the best performance I've *ever* / *never* been to.
5 *How* / *What* I liked / didn't like about it was …

5 ☆☆ **Read the review again. Answer the questions.**

1 Who is the concert for, in the reviewer's opinion?

___

2 What instruments do the musicians play?

___

PLAN

6 ☆☆ **Write your own review. First, take notes in your notebook about a music concert you have been to or seen on TV.**

Who was the concert for?
What was it like?
What did you like / not like about it?
Where did you see it?

7 **Decide what information to include in each paragraph. Use the information in Exercise 3 to help you.**

WRITE

8 ☆☆☆ **Write your review. Remember to include four paragraphs, the present perfect, and phrases from the *Useful Language* box (see Student's Book, p29).**

CHECK

9 **Do you …**

- say who it is for?
- describe the event?
- say what you liked / didn't like about it?

2 REVIEW

VOCABULARY

1 Complete the sentences with the words in the box.

architecture contemporary dance exhibition filmmaking gallery illustrations performance photography sculptures street art

1 Eduardo goes to the movies a lot because he's interested in ________________.
2 Lorenzo Quinn makes ________________ of people and things with different metals.
3 I love ________________, but you need a lot of energy and rhythm to move your body to the music.
4 The Louvre in Paris is the most famous art ________________ in the world – the *Mona Lisa* is there.
5 They saw a wonderful ________________ of paintings and sculptures by a local artist.
6 The ________________ in this book are in black and white, not color.
7 We saw a ________________ of *High School Musical* at our local theater – it was really good.
8 I bought a new camera for my ________________ class. I've taken some great pictures.
9 ________________ is an art because you need creativity to design, plan, and make buildings.
10 Some ________________ is OK, but I really don't like graffiti. It looks messy.

2 Read the definitions and complete the nouns.

1 o________________: a big group of musicians who play different instruments together
2 p________________: one of the people in a movie, play, or dance show
3 s________________: a part of a play or movie in which the action happens in one place
4 a________________: the group of people together in one place to watch or listen to a play, movie, etc.
5 a________________: a short performance that an actor, dancer, etc., gives to show they can play a particular part
6 l________________: the words of a song
7 r________________: the time when all the people in a play, dance, etc., practice to prepare for a performance
8 l________________: the words that an actor speaks when performing in a movie, play, etc.
9 s________________: a theater performance or a TV or radio program
10 r____________ s____________: a place where a musician makes and records their songs

GRAMMAR IN ACTION

3 Write questions and short answers (affirmative or negative) in the present perfect.

1 you / see the new Almodóvar movie? (✓)
____
2 he / take photos of his sculpture? (✓)
____
3 the visitors / come from all over the world? (✗)
____
4 she / ever sing in front of a big audience? (✗)
____
5 they / hear your new song? (✓)
____
6 you / have many exhibitions? (✗)
____
7 she / be to that gallery before? (✓)
____
8 the show / win many awards? (✗)
____

4 Make the sentences negative using the words in parentheses.

1 I've just done my homework. (not yet)

______

2 He's read that book already. (still not)

______

3 We've been to Venice. (still not)

______

4 The performance has just begun. (not yet)

______

5 The sculptor has explained his work. (still not)

______

6 We've just bought your new song. (not yet)

______

7 She's just met the photographer. (still not)

______

8 I've been into Paul's recording studio. (not yet)

______

CUMULATIVE GRAMMAR

5 Complete the conversation with the missing words. Circle the correct options.

INTERVIEWER Hello and welcome. We have some great music for you today, but I [1]_____ that one of our most talented young singers, Lexi West, is in the recording studio. Welcome to Miami, Lexi!

LEXI Thanks! It's great to be here. Actually, I [2]_____ an apartment in the city. It's all very new and exciting for me!

INTERVIEWER Yeah? Where [3]_____ live? You were born in Mexico, right? But of course you [4]_____ all over the world.

LEXI That's right. I [5]_____ back from New York, but while I [6]_____ and working abroad, I didn't have my own place. I [7]_____ with my parents.

INTERVIEWER Was there a lot of music in your home when you [8]_____, Lexi? I believe your father [9]_____ songs for you.

LEXI Yes, that's right. My dad was definitely my inspiration, but he was also very sensible. I [10]_____ on TV as a teenager, but he never let me miss school! I still [11]_____ his advice: it's OK to be ambitious, but don't get impatient!

INTERVIEWER Well, Lexi, you [12]_____ three number one hits, so you didn't have to wait very long to be famous!

	a	b	c
1	've still heard	haven't heard	've just heard
2	didn't buy	've just bought	was just buying
3	did you use to	were you used to	use you to
4	haven't traveled	've traveled	weren't traveling
5	was coming	have already come	've just come
6	was singing	wasn't singing	used to sing
7	didn't use to	was living	haven't lived
8	have grown up	grew up	were growing up
9	has just written	didn't use to write	used to write
10	performing	was performing	have just performed
11	used to forget	was forgetting	haven't forgotten
12	've already had	haven't had	were having

3 How do we communicate?

VOCABULARY

Communicating

1 ★ Put the letters in order to make words about communicating.

1 tereg g*reet*
2 retgesu g_ _ _ _ _ _
3 besiredc d_ _ _ _ _ _ _
4 ptreertin i_ _ _ _ _ _ _ _
5 stpo p_ _ _
6 eksha nsdah s_ _ _ _ h_ _ _ _
7 leims s_ _ _ _
8 vewa w_ _ _
9 latsenrta t_ _ _ _ _ _ _ _
10 wrheips w_ _ _ _ _ _
11 tsuho s_ _ _ _

2 ★★ Complete the sentences with words in Exercise 1.

1 A thumbs-up sign is a *gesture* that means "good."
2 I don't know what Jackie looks like. Can you ________ her to me?
3 Don't speak loudly. You'll wake up the baby. Please ________.
4 These instructions are in French. I need someone to ________ them for me.
5 There's Lucy across the street. Let's ________ at her. Maybe she will see us.
6 I only ________ when I'm very angry.
7 Everyone understands when you ________ at them. It means you're happy.
8 It's good to ________ comments online and then wait for people to reply to them.

3 ★★ Complete the spidergrams with the words in Exercise 1.

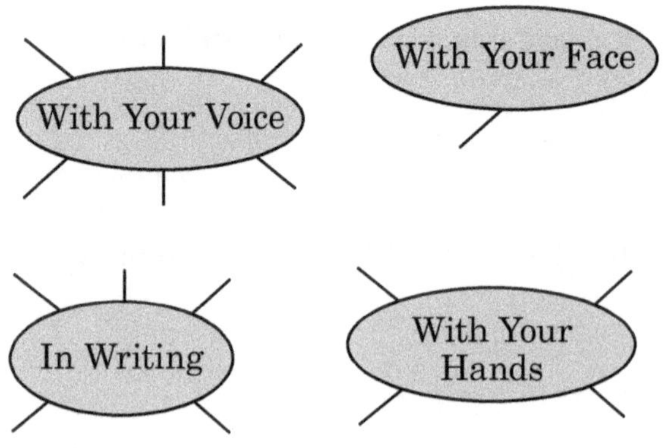

4 ★★ Complete the story with the correct form of words in Exercise 1.

I met my friend Kazue yesterday for the first time! Actually, I first met her online about six months ago. She's from Japan, and now she's visiting my country with her family. I [1] *greeted* her at the airport when she arrived. In her emails, she [2] ________ herself as pretty short, but in fact she's as tall as me. I also met her brother and her parents. I wanted to [3] ________ hands with them, but Kazue quietly [4] ________ in my ear that Japanese people don't usually do that when they meet. I already knew what her brother looked like because Kazue sometimes [5] ________ photos of him online. He was very friendly and he [6] ________ a lot. Kazue's parents don't speak English, but Kazue [7] ________ everything I said into Japanese. Kazue and her family were tired and wanted to go to their hotel. I arranged to meet Kazue the next day, and we [8] ________ goodbye as they drove away in a taxi.

Explore It!

Guess the correct answer.

People originally shook hands because …

a they wanted to find out how strong the other person was.
b they wanted to show that they didn't want to start a fight.
c they wanted to check that the other person had clean hands.

Find another interesting fact about greetings. Write a question and send it to a classmate in an email, or ask them in the next class.

READING

An Article

1 ☆ **Look at the photo. What emotions/actions do the emojis show?** ____________

2 ☆ **Read the article and complete the paragraphs (1–4) with the missing headings.**

From Japan to the World — Japan's Alphabets — The Most Popular Symbol — A World Language

3 ☆ **Find adverbs in the article with the meanings below.**

1 in a good way (paragraph 1) ____well____
2 with no problems (paragraph 2) ____________
3 very much (paragraph 3) ____________
4 not how you expect (paragraph 4) ____________

4 ☆☆ **Read the article again. Are the sentences *T* (true) or *F* (false)? Correct the false sentences.**

1 For verb endings like *-ing*, Japanese people use the *hiragana* alphabet.
T ____________
2 *Katakana* has the most symbols.
____
3 You can't use more than one alphabet in one text.
____
4 The first emojis didn't express many different feelings.
____
5 In paragraph C, "ones" refers to "people."
____
6 The writer hopes emojis will become an international language in the future.
____

5 ☆☆☆ **Answer the questions in your own words.**

1 Which emojis do you use most often? Why?
____
2 Apart from using emojis, how else can we show emotions in text messages?
____
3 Is the alphabet in your language different from English? If so, how?
____

Emojis

The World's Most Popular Alphabet?

1 ____________

Did you know that the Japanese language has three alphabets? One alphabet, *katakana*, is mostly for foreign words, like "pizza" (ピザ). This alphabet has 48 characters, or letters and symbols. Another alphabet, *hiragana*, is usually for grammar words, like the word ending "した," which changes a verb into the past tense – similar to *-ed* in English. *Hiragana* has 46 characters. A third alphabet, *kanji*, has about 50,000 different symbols. It is usually for verbs, adjectives, and nouns. For example, "山" is the Japanese symbol for "mountain." Often a piece of writing contains all three alphabets at the same time! Learning written Japanese well can be difficult!

2 ____________

But there is another kind of "alphabet" from Japan, which everyone can easily recognize. You probably use it a lot when you communicate with friends. It doesn't use letters; it uses emojis, which translates as "picture characters" in English. We can all recognize emojis when we see them. They show a huge range of feelings or actions, from love and sadness to dancing and waving.

3 ____________

The Japanese have used emojis since 1999. Of course, these early emojis were very simple, and people could only use them to show basic emotions. Since then, they have become more and more popular around the world, and the number of emoji symbols has greatly increased – now there are nearly 3,000 official ones. Everyone can understand emojis – it doesn't matter which country they are from.

4 ____________

And what is the most common emoji symbol that people use? Surprisingly, it is not a smiley face or a heart. It is the "tears of joy" emoji, showing a face laughing and crying happily. Perhaps in the future, there will be an emoji for every possible emotion, and we will be able to communicate with anyone in the world only by using emoji symbols!

GRAMMAR IN ACTION

Can, Could, Will Be Able To

1 ☆ Are these sentences about the *past*, *present*, or *future*?

1 Most people couldn't send each other quick messages 30 years ago. past
2 It's possible that we will be able to interpret any language on a smartphone app. ______
3 Animals can't communicate in the same way that humans can. ______
4 I couldn't speak until I was three years old. ______
5 I won't be able to use my phone in the mountains. ______

2 ☆☆ Complete the conversation with the correct form of *can*, *could*, or *will be able to* and the verbs in parentheses.

KIM [1] Can you tell (you / tell) me why you didn't reply to my email?
DAN Sorry! I was at my grandparents' house out in the country. I [2] ______ (not use) my phone.
KIM Really? But you [3] ______ (post) messages online. I saw them.
DAN Uh, yes, but I [4] ______ (not check) my email.
KIM OK, anyway, [5] ______ (you / help) me practice my presentation tomorrow for next week's test?
DAN Sorry, I [6] ______ (not do) it then. I'm really busy. I [7] ______ (help) you now, though.
KIM Oh, I [8] ______ (not practice) now. I haven't written anything yet.
DAN Well, we [9] ______ (write) it together now, if you want. What's the topic of the presentation?
KIM How to communicate successfully!

3 ☆☆ Complete the blogs with the correct words.

HOME ABOUT ME ARCHIVE FOLLOW

Julia

I [1] couldn't play the piano very well when I was younger. I didn't like practicing because the piano was in our living room downstairs. That meant everyone had to listen to me when I played, and no one [2] ______ watch TV or read. Now I have an electric piano and I [3] ______ use headphones. It's great because my family [4] ______ hear anything I'm playing! So now I'm practicing a lot, and I [5] ______ play very well.

Liam

I [6] ______ swim at all, but I'd like to. Last summer, I went with my friends to the beach, and I [7] ______ join in the fun in the water. That made me feel sad, so I hope I [8] ______ be able to start taking lessons in the next few months. I know that I [9] ______ be able to swim like a fish after just a few lessons, but I just want to be confident in the water so that I [10] ______ be able to swim with my friends next summer!

4 ☆☆☆ Look at the information about Vero. Write sentences with the correct form of *can*, *could*, and *will be able to*.

	1 play the piano	2 type quickly	3 sleep ten hours a night	4 ask her parents for money
when she was younger	✗		✓	
now	✓	✗	✗	✓
in the future		✓		✗

1 Vero couldn't play the piano when she was younger, but she can now.
2 ______
3 ______
4 ______

VOCABULARY AND LISTENING

A Radio Interview

3.01 **1 Listen to a radio interview about dolphins. Mark (✓) the topics that the people talk about.**

1 ☐ dolphin communication and language
2 ☐ dolphin greetings
3 ☐ the language of human babies
4 ☐ dolphin body language
5 ☐ how quickly dolphins can swim
6 ☐ new technology

3.01 **2 Listen again. Are the sentences *T* (true) or *F* (false)?**

1 Sara thinks that all dolphins speak the same language. F
2 Scientists believe dolphins have names. ___
3 Dolphins talk to each other at the same time without stopping. ___
4 In one experiment, two dolphins spoke on a phone. ___
5 Dolphins can communicate over long distances. ___
6 Scientists have the technology to translate what dolphins are saying. ___

Collocations with *To Say* and *To Tell*

3 Complete the flashcards with *to say* or *to tell*.

1 to say **hello**
2 ______ **sorry**
3 ______ **the truth**
4 ______ **a story**
5 ______ **a lie**
6 ______ **(someone) a secret**
7 ______ **yes / no**
8 ______ **(something) in Italian**
9 ______ **a joke**

4 Complete the sentences with the correct form of the collocations in Exercise 3.

1 Can I tell you a secret? But promise you won't tell anyone else.
2 How do you ______ "thank you" ______?
3 Let me ______ you a ______ about how I met my best friend.
4 The interviewer asked me if I wanted the job. I ______, of course!
5 Maria says she doesn't have any money, but I don't think she's ______. She always wears expensive clothes.
6 I ______ to your brother in the street, but he didn't hear me and he continued walking!
7 I like ______, but I can never make them sound funny.
8 I want to ______ for shouting at you last week.
9 Ed just ______ me a big ______. I'll never believe him again!

5 Answer the questions.

1 Have you ever told a "good" lie to help someone? What lie did you tell?
______
2 When you have a secret, who do you tell?
______
3 How many languages can you say something in? Which languages?
______

GRAMMAR IN ACTION

Present Perfect with *How long* ... ? and *For/Since*

1 ★ Circle the best ending for each sentence.

1 I've lived here for …
 (a) two years. b I was 14 years old.
2 I've had this phone for …
 a a long time. b 2015.
3 I haven't eaten anything since …
 a about three hours. b this morning.
4 I've been able to speak French since …
 a ten years. b I was a child.
5 My best friend and I have known each other for …
 a six years. b we started school together.
6 Max has been on the computer since …
 a all day. b he woke up.

2 ★★ Complete the questions with *How long* and the present perfect form of the verbs in the box.

be	have	know	like	~~live~~

A [1] How long have you lived here?
B For about six months. I really like it here. It's a nice city.
A So, Emma and Kirsty are friends?
[2] ____________ each other?
B Since they were about three years old. They've been best friends for ages!
A I didn't know Olivia liked watching tennis.
[3] ____________ it?
B For a long time. She's played on the school team since she was really young.
A I see that Will has a new bike.
[4] ____________ it?
B For about a week. He needed a new one. The old one was too small for him.
A I'm sorry I'm late, everyone.
[5] ____________ here?
B Not long. Don't worry. We only got here ten minutes ago.

Present Perfect and Simple Past

3 ★★ Complete the joke with the simple past or present perfect form of the verbs in parentheses.

My friend [1] told (tell) me a funny joke this morning. I [2] ____________ (hear) a lot of jokes in my life, but this one [3] ____________ (make) me laugh when I [4] ____________ (hear) it.
A girl and her father [5] ____________ (be) at the dinner table having some soup. The girl [6] ____________ (ask) her dad, "Dad, are spiders good to eat?" "What a horrible question," [7] ____________ (say) her dad. "Can't you think of anything nice to say at dinnertime? Please let me eat. I [8] ____________ (not eat) anything since this morning!" The girl [9] ____________ (decide) to be quiet. They both [10] ____________ (eat) their dinner in silence. Later, the girl's father [11] ____________ (ask), "Why did you want to know about spiders earlier?" She replied, "Oh, there was a spider in your soup. But it [12] ____________ (go) now."

4 ★★ Write questions with the present perfect or the simple past.

1 a you / ever / tell / a lie? Have you ever told a lie?
 b Who / you / tell / the lie to?
 ____
 c Why / you / tell / it?
 ____
2 a anyone / ever / tell / you a secret?
 ____
 b it / a very big secret?
 ____
 c you / ever / tell / another person the secret?
 ____

5 ★★★ Choose question 1 or 2 from Exercise 4. Write your answers.

____
____

WRITING

A Listicle

1 ☆ Read the listicle and (circle) the best title.

1 How to Communicate with People from Other Countries
2 How to Be a Good Language Learner
3 How to Be a Better Communicator
4 How to Tell Jokes

Over the last few years, I've learned a few things, and now I can communicate much better than before. Here are my top five tips.

- **Use Body Language**

Use your hands and gesture to make a point, and always make eye contact. Since I started doing this, people have paid a lot more attention to me!

- **Use Intonation**

Your tone of voice, that is, how it sounds, shows your feelings. If your voice sounds flat and bored, your listener will be bored, too! Before, I didn't use to think about intonation, but now I understand that how you say something is very important.

- **Be a Good Listener**

Good communicators listen. Of course, say what you want to say, but later on, ask questions to find out what the other person is thinking.

- **Be Yourself!**

Most people can tell when someone is telling a lie. All my life, I've never been very confident or sociable. Be honest and don't try to appear more confident than you really are. Always be yourself.

- **Tell Jokes**

Smile and try to find the funny side whenever you can – this will make your listener more relaxed. This is especially important these days, when the world can be such a serious place.

Try to use some of these helpful tips and you'll soon be able to see the difference it makes!

2 ☆☆ Read the listicle again and complete the sentences.

1 People pay more attention to you when you *use your hands and gesture, and make eye contact.*
2 ________________ lets the listener know how you are feeling.
3 Good communicators listen and ________________.
4 It's a bad idea to not tell the truth when you meet people because ________________ ________________.
5 Telling jokes helps the listener be ________________.

3 ☆☆ (Circle) the correct meanings for the *Useful Language* words and phrases.

1 **over the last few years** *(recently) / since I was a baby*
2 **since** *at the moment / from a specific time in the past*
3 **before** *earlier / after some time has passed*
4 **later on** *after some time has passed / recently*
5 **all my life** *at the moment / since I was born*
6 **these days** *at the moment / earlier*
7 **soon** *earlier / in the very near future*

PLAN

4 ☆☆ Write your own listicle. Choose one of the other titles from Exercise 1 and take notes in your notebook. Use these headings.

Title:

Introduction:

A List of Five Tips

A Short Ending

WRITE

5 ☆☆☆ Write your listicle. Remember to include an introduction, five tips and a short ending, *can*, *could*, *will be able to*, the correct past tenses, and words and phrases from the *Useful Language* box (see Student's Book, p41).

CHECK

6 Do you …

- have an introduction that will interest the reader?
- have an ending to make the reader think?

3 REVIEW

VOCABULARY

1 Circle the correct words.

People [1]*greet / gesture* each other in many ways when they meet. All around the world, it's very common to [2]*whisper / wave* when you want to attract someone's attention and then simply [3]*smile / shout* to show that you are happy. If we don't do this, then the other person might [4]*interpret / translate* your serious face as meaning that you don't want to meet them. Perhaps the most common way to say hello in Europe and North America is to [5]*wave / shake hands*. In other places, like Japan, people bow (move their head and body forward). In the Philippines, some people perform a [6]*gesture / shake* called *mano* (this Spanish word [7]*posts / translates* to "hand" in English), putting the other person's hand on their head. In some cultures, people put their noses together when they meet. In Costa Rica, however, people [8]*shout / whisper* "Oooooooopppe!" in a very loud voice when they meet!

2 Complete the sentences with the correct form of *to say* or *to tell*.

1 Can I __________ you a secret?
2 I'd like to know how to __________ "I love you" in Italian.
3 When you don't want to do something, you can always __________ no.
4 I know I said I was 16, but I wasn't __________ the truth.
5 Paula didn't __________ hello to me at the party.
6 George __________ me the story of how his parents met. It was really funny.
7 I'm not very good at __________ lies – my face always turns red!
8 Fernando __________ a really terrible joke and no one laughed.

GRAMMAR IN ACTION

3 Mark (✓) the correct sentences and correct five incorrect sentences

1 I can swim when I was only two years old. ☐
____
2 I think I can be able to get a good job in the future. ☐
____
3 I couldn't come to the party last night because I was sick. ☐
____
4 Will you be able to call me when you get home? ☐
____
5 I can't speak English until I went to school. ☐
____
6 Can you watch TV late at night on the weekend? ☐
____
7 The school will be able let me know about my test score next week. ☐
____
8 Now I could speak Italian well, but in the past I couldn't. ☐
____

4 **Complete the sentences with the simple past or present perfect form of the verbs in parentheses.**

1 I ____________________ (live) in London for about ten years – I love it here.
2 Before you came to London, how long ____________________ (you / live) in New York?
3 It ____________________ (be) 50 years since the first man stepped on the moon.
4 They ____________________ (not learn) much Russian in Moscow – they were only there for two months.
5 My sister ____________________ (not finish) reading that book, but she will soon.
6 I ____________________ (not do) any exercise last week, so I want to do a lot this week.
7 You and Frank get along really well. How long ____________________ (you / know) him?
8 I can't play soccer this afternoon because I ____________________ (fall) off my bike yesterday.

CUMULATIVE GRAMMAR

5 **Complete the text with the missing words. Circle the correct options.**

[1] ____ heard the story *The Boy Who Cried Wolf*? The parents of a young boy asked him to take care of their sheep on a lonely mountain. The boy [2] ____ yes, but he soon found that it was a very boring job. After about four hours, he decided to do something interesting. He started shouting, "Help! Wolf!" There [3] ____ no wolf, of course, but his parents came running.

"Where's the wolf?" they asked.

"Sorry!" said the boy, "I [4] ____."

The parents [5] ____ very angry and went back to the village. A few hours [6] ____ and then suddenly the boy saw a real wolf! "Help! Wolf!" he shouted. But this time, no one came. They thought it was a joke again! This [7] ____ an old story, but the message is still relevant. For example, once I [8] ____ to go to school, so I told my parents I was sick. I don't [9] ____ tell lies, so they believed me, and I didn't go to school that day. But unfortunately, the next week, I really was sick. My parents didn't believe me this time, and I [10] ____ stay at home – I felt terrible! I [11] ____ lied since then! So remember: don't cry wolf because you [12] ____ get help when you really need to!

	a	b	c
1	Have you ever	Have ever you	Haven't you never
2	is saying	said	told
3	is	were	was
4	was joking	joke	have joked
5	was	were	have been
6	are passing	have passed	passed
7	has been	is being	is
8	didn't want	didn't wanted	couldn't want
9	usually	never	sometimes
10	won't be able	couldn't	can't
11	don't	didn't	haven't
12	can't	couldn't	won't be able to

4 How can I stay healthy?

VOCABULARY

Health and Fitness

1 ☆ **Complete the words and phrases with the vowels (a, e, i, o, u).**

1 sw*e* *a*t
2 c_ _gh
3 r_l_x
4 tr_ _n
5 sn_ _z_
6 g_t b_tt_r
7 g_ j_gg_ng
8 h_v_ _ f_v_r
9 g_t s_ck
10 g_t str_ss_d
11 w_rm _p
12 w_rk _ _t
13 g_t _n_ _gh sl_ _p

2 ☆ **Mark the words and phrases that are in the correct column (✓) and those that are in the incorrect column (✗). Then write one extra word for each column.**

HEALTH		FITNESS	
1 *cough*	✓	7 *go jogging*	☐
2 *get better*	☐	8 *have a fever*	☐
3 *work out*	☐	9 *train*	☐
4 *relax*	☐	10 *sneeze*	☐
5 *warm up*	☐	11 *get enough sleep*	☐
6 ______		12 ______	

3 ☆☆ **Complete the sentences with the correct form of the words in Exercise 1.**

1 Is it true that you can't *sneeze* with your eyes open?
2 Sam is ______ for a half marathon at the moment.
3 A Isabel can't come today. She's not feeling very well.
B Oh, no! I hope she ______ soon!
4 He ______ a lot when he exercises. His clothes get very wet!
5 Remember to ______ before you run or do exercise, especially in cold weather.
6 Don't ______ about your exams – relax, you'll be OK!

4 ☆☆ **Circle the correct options.**

CARO Hey, Leo! Do you want to go [1]*jogging* / *sweating* in the park? Meet me there?

LEO Sorry, I can't. I'm getting [2]*better* / *stressed* about my exams.

CARO Oh, come on! Working [3]*out* / *in* will be good for you!

LEO I have a [4]*sneeze* / *fever*, too. I'm really hot and I feel terrible.

CARO Oh, no! But it isn't a good idea to do schoolwork if you want to get [5]*better* / *stressed*.

LEO I know … anyway, you're [6]*training* / *relaxing* for the marathon – it's very difficult to run with you! ☹

CARO OK. Get enough [7]*exercise* / *sleep*. Don't study all night!

LEO OK, and don't forget to [8]*work out* / *warm up* before running. You hurt your leg last time!

Explore It!

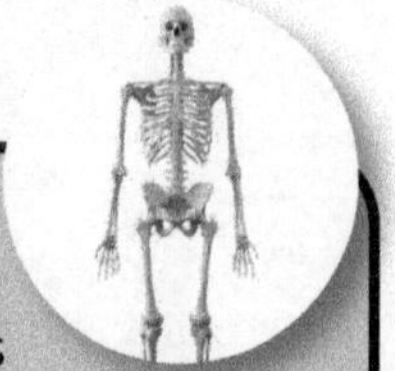

Guess the correct answer.

Almost half of all the bones in the human body are in the …

a hands and feet.
b legs and arms.
c head and back.

Find another interesting fact about exercise and the human body. Write a question and send it to a classmate in an email, or ask them in the next class.

READING

Online FAQs

1 ☆ **Match the photos (a–d) with the FAQs and answers (1–4).**

a
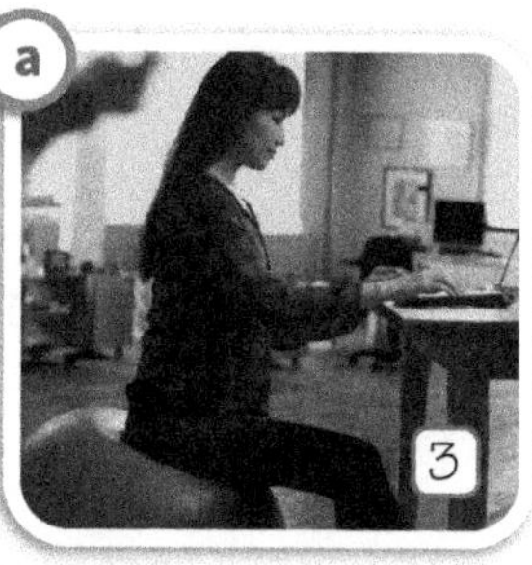

b

c

d

Home | News | FAQs

Read some of our FAQs about staying fit and healthy during the school week and study sessions.

1 **Q** What can I do to get active during a school day and when can I do it?

A Getting exercise on a school day can be easy. Not enough people cycle or walk to and from school. And if that takes too much of your time, then use your lunch break to exercise or join a sports team after school.

2 **Q** I spend too much time sitting at a desk and not enough time on my feet. What can I do?

A We spend too many hours sitting at a desk or in front of a **screen**. Standing up exercises many different **muscles**. These muscles can become **weak** when we don't use them enough. You can now buy **adjustable** desks, which you can make higher so you can stand up while working. It's a good idea to stand and walk around every half an hour during long study sessions.

3 **Q** What are fitness balls and how can they help me?

A Some people say they feel too silly sitting on a big plastic ball. But fitness balls are a great way to work out, as they help build the muscles in your **back** and **stomach** … all while you're sitting down! A fitness ball for home study is perfect for long hours sitting at a desk.

4 **Q** There is too much noise and stress in my life. How can I get a little quiet time?

A One word: yoga. The practice of yoga is thousands of years old, and when you find a little time between studying and exams to relax in this way, you can concentrate better. It's free and it's easy to do alone!

GET MORE INFORMATION HERE

2 ☆☆ **Match the words in bold in the online FAQs with the meanings.**

1 you need these to carry heavy objects *muscles*
2 the opposite of strong ______
3 where food goes in the body ______
4 the part of a computer where you see words or pictures ______
5 if something is this, you can change it to make it better ______
6 the part of the body that is opposite to the front ______

3 ☆☆ **Read the online FAQs again and answer the questions.**

1 What times of the day can students do exercise, according to the FAQs?
before and after school and at lunchtime
2 What can happen to the body when we don't stand up regularly?
______
3 How often do you need to move around when studying?
______
4 Why is the fitness ball unpopular with some people?
______
5 How can a fitness ball help your body?
______
6 Which activity can students do to relax, according to the FAQs?
______

4 ☆☆☆ **Answer the questions.**

1 Which of the things in the FAQs have you tried?
______
2 Think of one more FAQ about young people's health and fitness.
______

GRAMMAR IN ACTION

Quantifiers

1 ★ Complete the sentences with *much* or *many*.

1 Kylie did too _much_ exercise yesterday and now she's very tired.
2 Is it possible to have too ________ fun on the weekend?
3 There were too ________ people in the pool, so we didn't swim.
4 Everyone I know has too ________ work to take a vacation.
5 Skiing costs too ________ money for most students.
6 Too ________ students get stressed at exam time.

2 ★ Match the beginnings of the sentences (1–6) with the ends (a–f).

1 Swimming is great, but only a few [c]
2 Please give me a little more [ ]
3 Relaxing is hard: I need a little [ ]
4 The nearest gym is a few [ ]
5 It's very hot, so take a little [ ]
6 Stand up for just a few [ ]

a minutes every half an hour.
b kilometers away.
c schools have swimming pools.
d water with you.
e help from my yoga teacher.
f time to finish my homework.

3 ★★ Put the words in the correct order to make sentences.

1 long / school / aren't / enough / days / Normal
Normal school days aren't long enough.
2 noisy / My / too / friend's / are / dogs
____
3 enough / I'm / drive / can't / not / because / I / old
____
4 her / Gisela / desk / too / says / low / is
____
5 everyone / aren't / chairs / for / There / enough
____

4 ★★ Match the meanings (a–e) with the sentences (1–5) in Exercise 3.

a He/She's too young. [3]
b They're not quiet enough. [ ]
c There are too many people. [ ]
d They are too short. [ ]
e It's not high enough. [ ]

5 ★★★ Complete the online post and its response with the phrases in the box.

a few problems	enough strength	
not enough answers	not enough options	
~~too many questions~~	too old	too young (x2)

Young Teen Health **FORUM**

Posts:

I'd like to see more advice about health and fitness for boys on this website. There are [1] _too many questions_ from teenage girls and [2] ________ for boys. What advice can you give young male teens for a regular workout?
Andrés

Thanks for your comment, Andrés! Teenage boys can also have [3] ________ with their body image as they are growing up and changing. Fitness for boys is easy when you're young, but the early teenage years can be complicated. You feel you're [4] ________ to play silly games with friends but [5] ________ to work out at the gym with older guys. Perhaps you don't have [6] ________ yet to join an adult sports team. But you're never [7] ________ to exercise regularly. If there are [8] ________ where you live, think about running or parkour, or working out at home. Hope this helps!

VOCABULARY AND LISTENING An Interview

Healthy Eating

1 ☆ **Complete the puzzle. Use the clues.**

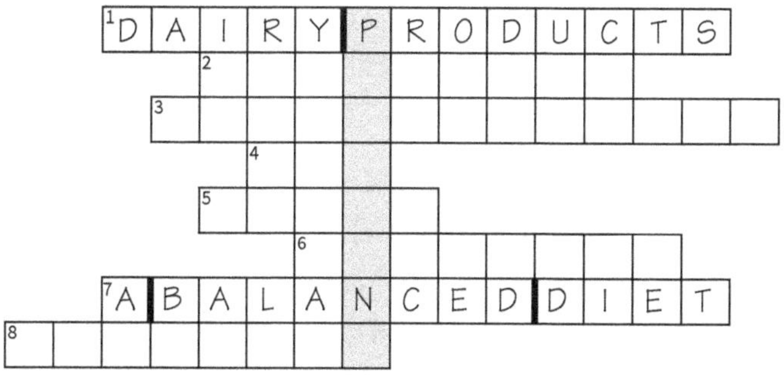

1 These foods usually come from milk.
2 You can study this to learn about food and a healthy diet.
3 We get most of our energy from these. You find them in bread and pasta.
4 There is a lot of this in cheese and chocolate.
5 This helps food pass through the body.
6 We get these natural substances from fruit (C) and sunlight (D).
7 This is a good mixture of many food types.
8 We count these to find out how much energy there is in our food.

2 ☆ **Circle the correct definition for the secret word (in gray) in Exercise 1.**

a They help your bones grow longer.
b They help your body grow stronger.
c They help your heart work.

4.01 **3** ☆☆ **<u>Underline</u> the words that are the same or similar in your language – notice any differences in spelling. Then listen to the English pronunciation.**

1 A balance between mental and physical health is important.
2 We know that calcium is good for our bones.
3 Do you know why grains are good for you?
4 Basketball practice always ends with a fun activity.

4.02 **4** ☆☆ **Listen to an interview about "Blue Zones." Number the topics the speakers mention in the order you hear them (1–4).**

a ☐ regular exercise
b ☐ the Mediterranean diet
c [1] centenarians
d ☐ eating food from the ocean

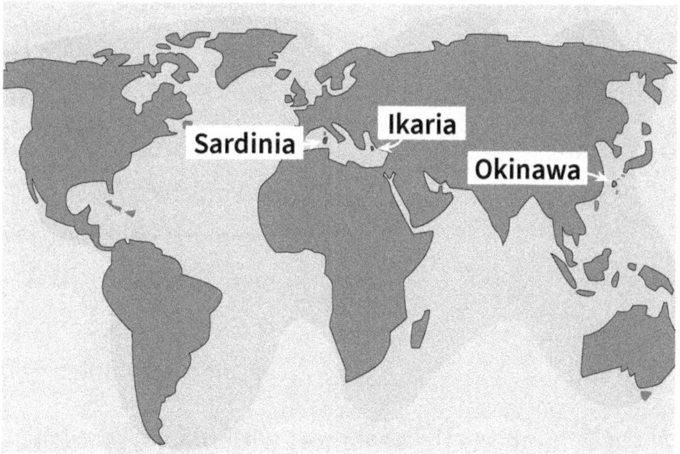

4.02 **5** ☆☆ **Listen again and circle the correct answers.**

1 A Blue Zone is a place where people often ... .
 a become large.
 b live to an old age.
 c eat seafood.
2 Philippa was surprised because many Blue Zones are ... .
 a very big.
 b in Asia.
 c islands.
3 The food tofu is very high in ... .
 a carbohydrates.
 b calories.
 c protein.
4 Philippa says people in the Mediterranean often eat ... .
 a too much meat.
 b very little fat.
 c a lot of sweet things.
5 Philippa thinks that ... also important for a long life.
 a family and friends are
 b working outside is
 c getting up early is

GRAMMAR IN ACTION

Should, Shouldn't, and Ought To

1 ★ **Look at the photos. Complete the sentences with *should* or *shouldn't* and the correct verb.**

1 
2 
3 
4 
5 
6 

1 You __should eat__ enough fruit.
2 You ____________ too much coffee.
3 You ____________ too much chocolate.
4 You ____________ enough fish.
5 You ____________ too many sweet drinks.
6 You ____________ enough vegetables.

2 ★★ **Complete the sentences with *should*, *shouldn't*, or *ought*.**

1 If you're always late for class, you __should__ get up earlier.
2 People who can't get up ________ go to bed so late.
3 Ilona can't relax: I think she ________ to do yoga.
4 Our teacher said we ________ to eat our lunch outside because it's hot today.
5 You ________ give chocolate to dogs – it's bad for them.
6 We ________ eat more tofu because it's full of protein.

3 ★★ **Underline and correct one mistake in each sentence.**

1 You don't look well; perhaps you shouldn't see a doctor. __should__
2 Our fridge is empty, so we ought go to the store. ________
3 You should worry so much about your exams. ________
4 What should I to do to get healthier? ________
5 He oughts to eat more protein. ________
6 You shouldn't to eat unhealthy food if you want to live to be 100. ________

4 ★★★ **Complete the article with the phrases in the box.**

ought to check ~~ought to know~~ ought to start should be should drink should take shouldn't carry shouldn't spend

Top Tips for a Road Trip – By Bike!

Planning a road trip by bike? Here's what you [1] __ought to know__ to stay fit and healthy!

Your bike [2] ____________ light enough because if it's too heavy, cycling becomes difficult in hot weather. But you [3] ____________ that it's big enough for you – a bike that's too small soon gets uncomfortable.

You [4] ____________ too many things with you. Too many bags slow you down, so you [5] ____________ two small bags, maximum.

You [6] ____________ a lot of water, so take a one-liter water bottle.

You [7] ____________ too much money on maps: paper maps are heavy. Download maps onto your smartphone before you leave home. And finally, you [8] ____________ early in the day – before it gets too hot!

5 ★★★ **Choose one of the topics in the box and write three pieces of advice in your notebook. Use *should*, *ought to*, and *shouldn't*.**

eating more healthily
preparing for an exam
writing an essay

WRITING

A Post on a Forum

1 ☆ **Read the post on a forum and the response. Who does Carlos want to help? What does Tom suggest?**

____

Forum:
We ♥ Animals

Posts:

Carlos: My grandma lives alone now. She sits and thinks about the past and gets stressed about her health. I think she ought to get a cat or a dog, but she thinks she's too old. What do you think?

Tom@the Den: Hey, great that you've written to me – thanks! We all have stress in our lives and especially old people living alone. Pets make people feel happier and more relaxed. In fact, did you know that they can also help with stress? Have you ever tried sitting with a cat or walking a dog when you're stressed? It really helps! Why? Stress often causes high blood pressure, and just being near an animal can help lower it. I think your grandma should definitely try having a pet. If she likes dogs, for example, but doesn't want to keep a dog as a pet, I can recommend trying a therapy dog. There are specially trained dogs that can visit old people with their owners or volunteers. Your grandma can enjoy the dog without worrying about it! Why don't you look online for a therapy pet center near you? Or you could always ask at your local vet – they ought to be able to help. That way, your grandma can relax and beat stress.

2 ☆☆ **Read the post and response again. Answer the questions.**

1 Why doesn't Carlos's grandma want a pet?
She thinks she's too old.

2 How can pets help with stress?
____

3 Why is a therapy pet a better option for Carlos's grandma?
____

4 Where should Carlos find out about a therapy pet?
____

3 ☆☆ **Circle the correct options in the *Useful Language* phrases. Then check in the forum response.**

1 You *would* / *could* always ask …
2 Have you ever tried *sitting* / *sit* … ?
3 *This* / *That* way, your grandma can relax …
4 Why *don't* / *not* you look … ?
5 I can recommend *to try* / *trying* …

PLAN

4 ☆☆ **Write your own response to a post on a forum. Use the problem below or your own ideas. Take notes.**

Please help! I drink two liters of soda a day! I know it's bad for me, but I think I'm addicted to the sugar and caffeine! What can I do?

Advice: ______________________

Reasons: ______________________

WRITE

5 ☆☆☆ **Write your response. Remember to include a greeting and thanks, *should*, *shouldn't*, *ought to*, quantifiers, and phrases from the *Useful Language* box (see Student's Book, p53).**

CHECK

6 **Do you …**

- give advice with reasons?
- use an informal style?

4 REVIEW

VOCABULARY

1 Look at the photos and (circle) the correct options.

2 Match the beginnings of the sentences (1–8) with the ends (a–h).

1 Nutrition is the food we eat ☐
2 Hamburgers, ice cream, and chocolate ☐
3 The number of calories in food ☐
4 Carbohydrates give us ☐
5 Protein helps our bodies ☐
6 Fruit and vegetables contain ☐
7 A balanced diet ☐
8 A lot of fiber is good for the stomach ☐

a tells us how much energy it has.
b grow and be healthy and strong.
c a lot of vitamins A and C.
d and how our body uses it.
e the energy we need to move.
f have a lot of fat in them.
g and travels through the body quickly.
h is eating a good variety of healthy food.

GRAMMAR IN ACTION

3 (Circle) the correct options.

1 Is there *little* / *enough* food for everyone, or should I cook more?
2 We don't use too *many* / *much* milk products in our restaurant.
3 Owen's just gone out to buy *a few* / *a little* eggs.
4 We all need to relax and have *much* / *a little* fun.
5 My baby sister isn't *old enough* / *enough old* to make her own breakfast.
6 This article gives you *a little* / *few* ideas on healthy diets.

1 *sneeze* / *cough*

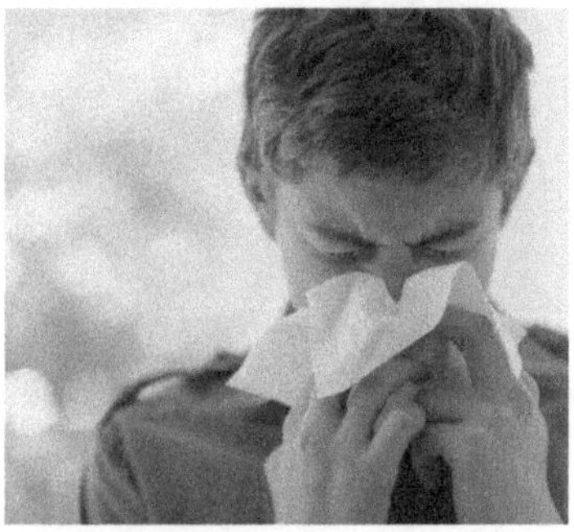

2 *sneeze* / *cough*

3 *go jogging* / *warm up*

4 *relax* / *get sick*

5 *warm up* / *sweat*

6 *have a fever* / *get enough sleep*

7 *sweat* / *warm up*

8 *get stressed* / *get enough sleep*

4 Complete the sentences with *should*, *shouldn't*, or *ought*.

1 What ________ we eat to grow stronger?

2 The children ________ to eat fewer chips and candy.

3 A balanced diet ________ to have a little of everything.

4 You ________ drink coffee at night – it stops you from sleeping.

5 How much exercise ________ we do?

6 You ________ eat more than you need.

CUMULATIVE GRAMMAR

5 Complete the conversation with the missing words. Circle the correct options.

INTERVIEWER You've just completed a marathon; well done! I'm sure you're tired, but [1] ______ to answer a few questions?

BERNADETTE Sure, I just need [2] ______ water. OK, so yeah, it was a great run.

INTERVIEWER It was! You [3] ______ a runner, did you? Tell us how it started.

BERNADETTE I often got sick when I was younger, and I wasn't [4] ______ to play sports.

INTERVIEWER That's hard to believe! You've [5] ______ a marathon in record time!

BERNADETTE As a child, I spent [6] ______ time in bed, and I really wasn't fit at all.

INTERVIEWER Not enough young people exercise as much as they [7] ______ to. What changed for you?

BERNADETTE One day, my mother [8] ______ a TV show about foods that some people [9] ______ eat because it makes them sick. We later discovered that I [10] ______ eat bread or anything with gluten in it.

INTERVIEWER And what [11] ______ then?

BERNADETTE I changed my diet right, and I [12] ______ gluten since then. I felt better, started playing sports, and the rest is history!

	a	b	c
1	can you	will you be able	should you
2	too much	a few	a little
3	didn't use to be	used not be	didn't use be
4	enough strong	too strong	strong enough
5	just completed	still completed	yet completed
6	enough	too little	too much
7	should	ought	shouldn't
8	is seeing	has seen	saw
9	can't	can't to	can
10	shouldn't to	shouldn't	ought to
11	happens	happen	happened
12	didn't eat	haven't eaten	still didn't eat

5 How can we save our planet?

VOCABULARY

Planet Earth

1 ☆ **Complete the crossword. Use the clues.**

DOWN ↓

1 We usually separate our paper, plastic, and food … into different trash cans.

2 I try to save … at home – I always turn off the lights when I'm not using them.

3 Cycling or walking is better for the … than traveling by car.

5 Governments want to reduce the carbon … (or CO_2) that their countries produce.

8 We all live on … Earth.

ACROSS →

4 Tigers are an … species. It's possible they will all die in a few years.

6 There used to be a lot of … near here, like birds and butterflies, but not now.

7 Trees produce … for us to breathe.

8 Traffic causes a lot of air … in cities.

9 … change causes hotter weather around the world.

10 … power from the sun produces a lot of electricity.

11 Plastic in the ocean is bad for all … life, from large whales to small fish.

Explore It!

Guess the correct answer.

How much of the plastic that we use every year ends up in the seas and oceans?

a 1 percent b 5 percent c 10 percent

Find another interesting fact about pollution in the ocean. Write a question and send it to a classmate in an email, or ask them in the next class.

2 ☆☆ **Complete the notes with words from Exercise 1.**

Things We Should Reduce

- the amount of carbon [1] dioxide that we produce
- [2] ______ (e.g., air, water, and noise)
- [3] ______ (e.g., plastic and food)
- the effects of [4] ______ change (e.g., rising temperatures and sea levels)
- the amount of [5] ______ that we use (e.g., electricity and gas)

Things We Need to Protect or Save

- the [6] ______ (the air, our water, etc.)
- [7] ______ life (e.g., fish)
- [8] ______ Earth (our home – we only have one!)
- all animals, but especially [9] ______ species (e.g., tigers and gorillas)

3 ☆☆☆ **Circle the correct words.**

We face many environmental problems, such as rising levels of [1]*carbon* / *oxygen* dioxide in the air, which cause [2]*climate* / *planet* change. Plastic is also a big cause of [3]*pollution* / *energy*. Every year, we put a lot of plastic [4]*energy* / *waste* into our oceans. This is a huge problem for [5]*endangered* / *marine* life. It ends up in the stomachs of fish, which bigger animals then eat, including us. Many animals are therefore becoming [6]*endangered* / *marine*. But plastic is all over the [7]*planet* / *environment*. Even high mountains now have millions of tiny pieces of plastic on them, carried there by the wind.

READING

A News Story

1 ☆ **Look at the photos and read the news story quickly. Circle the best title.**

a Why We Should Use Drinking Straws

b The History of Drinking Straws

c The End of Drinking Straws?

News

Search

Home News Articles Sign In Register

Most of us have used straws. They are useful and [1] c. When we get a soda or juice from a café or restaurant, for example, it often comes with a straw, [2] ______. We usually use them once and then **dispose of** them immediately. In fact, people in the U.S.A. use 500 million every day. That's enough straws to go around the planet 2.5 times!

The big problem with straws is that many of them [3] ______. Europeans **recycle** only about 30 percent of their plastic, and straws are in the top ten **items** of **litter** found on beaches every year.

The good news is that [4] ______. More and more big companies are deciding not to use straws, or to provide them only when customers have asked for them. The city of Seattle, in the U.S.A., has already put a **ban** on straws, and the European Union wants to do the same by 2030. England plans to do this in 2020. Even the British Queen [5] ______.

So, it is possible that plastic drinking straws will soon be a thing of the past. Many people believe that we can continue to protect our environment by also reducing all the other plastic objects that we only use once, [6] ______.

2 ☆☆ **Complete the article with the missing sentence parts (a–f).**

a end up in the ocean, as waste

b such as bags, cups, and bottles

~~c they can be fun to drink with~~

d people are starting to do something about the problem

e including when we haven't asked for one

f has decided not to have plastic straws in any of her houses

3 ☆☆ **Match the words in bold in the news story with the definitions.**

1 things on a list items

2 put something in the trash can after we have used it ______

3 an official law that stops something from happening ______

4 use something again, or change it into something different ______

5 small pieces of trash in public places ______

4 ☆☆ **What do these numbers in the news story describe?**

1 30 percent is the amount of plastic that Europeans recycle

2 500 million ______

3 2.5 ______

4 2020 ______

5 10 ______

5 ☆☆☆ **Apart from a ban, how can we reduce the number of plastic straws people use? Write three ideas.**

______

______

______

GRAMMAR IN ACTION

The First Conditional

1 ☆ **Circle the correct options.**

1 If I (see) / *don't* see any litter on the beach, I'll pick it up.

2 I won't use my bike tomorrow *unless* / *if* it's raining. I don't want to get wet.

3 Unless we *use* / *don't use* alternative forms of energy, we will create more air pollution.

4 If you *will leave* / *leave* your computer on all night, it will waste energy.

5 Some cities *may* / *may be* underwater if sea levels rise.

6 I'll travel by train if I *go* / *might go* on vacation this year.

2 ☆☆ **Complete the sentences with the phrases in the box.**

climate change will get worse
if we stop using so much plastic
~~it will help the planet~~
many types of plants may be in danger
there might be more plastic than fish by 2050
unless we protect them

1 If we reduce our energy use,
it will help the planet ________.

2 Many animals could become endangered
____
________.

3 If we lose a lot of insect species,
____
________.

4 If we don't reduce the amount of carbon dioxide,
____
________.

5 Unless we stop polluting our oceans,
____
________.

6 It will help the planet
____
________.

3 ☆☆ **Complete the text with the verbs in the box.**

act continue is might be
~~might not see~~ will need

If you drive somewhere on a summer night and check the front window of your car after, you [1] *might not see* many dead insects on it. This doesn't sound like a problem. In fact, if your car [2] ________ clean, you will probably be pleased. However, this is a worrying sign. Over the last 30 years, the number of insects has fallen by 75 percent. But if there are fewer flies and mosquitoes in the future, the world [3] ________ a better place, right? Wrong! The problem is that if insects [4] ________ to disappear, we will all be in trouble. Many plants depend on them. As insects move from one plant to another, they carry pollen, which helps plants grow again. And if the number of people on the planet keeps on rising, we [5] ________ more and more food. Unless we [6] ________ quickly, insect numbers could fall even more. This could be very bad news for both humans and the planet.

4 ☆☆☆ **Complete the second sentence so that it has a similar meaning to the first. Use the word in parentheses.**

1 If we don't do something soon, it's possible that endangered species will disappear.
Endangered species could disappear if we don't do something soon. (could)

2 There will be huge problems if we don't protect our environment.
________ our environment, there will be huge problems. (unless)

3 If we don't stop using chemicals on farms, it's possible that insect numbers will fall.
________ if we don't stop using chemicals on farms. (might)

4 If we do something now, we might stop climate change.
Unless we do something now, we ________ climate change. (might)

5 ☆☆☆ **Complete the sentences with your own ideas.**

1 Unless we do something about climate change,
________.

2 We might be able to help the planet if
________.

VOCABULARY AND LISTENING

Natural Environments

1 ★ Look at the photos and complete the natural environment words.

1 bay

2 v______

3 c______

4 c______

5 c______

6 i______

7 r______

8 s______

9 v______

10 w______

2 ★ Choose the three most difficult words to remember in Exercise 1. Then draw a picture of each one in your notebook (see the *Learn to Learn* tip in the Student's Book, p62).

3 ★★ Circle the correct options.

1 A *stream* (circled) / *bay* is a small river, usually in the country.
2 You only find *icebergs* / *cliffs* in very cold places like the Arctic.
3 A *valley* / *cave* is a big hole in a mountain or under the ground.
4 A *cliff* / *valley* is a high area of vertical rock, often near the ocean.
5 A *stream* / *waterfall* is where a river falls from a high point to a lower point.
6 A *volcano* / *bay* is a mountain with a hole at the top. Sometimes gases and hot liquids come out.
7 A *rainforest* / *waterfall* is a hot place with trees and a lot of animals.
8 A *bay* / *valley* is an area between hills or mountains. There is often a river at the bottom.

A Class Discussion

4 ★ (5.01) Listen to the class discussion. Which four natural environments in Exercise 1 do the students mention?

1 ______ 2 ______
3 ______ 4 ______

5 ★★ (5.01) Listen again and complete the notes.

Harry talks about caves in [1] New Zealand. Inside the caves there is a small [2] ______. To travel through the caves, you need to take a [3] ______. If you look up at the top of the cave, you can see thousands of [4] ______ – they look like stars.

Abbie talks about [5] ______ in Papua New Guinea – these are very difficult to get to. There are also rainforests where scientists have found a lot of [6] ______. They have discovered a colorful fish, a river [7] ______, and a tree kangaroo. There are only [8] ______ tenkile tree kangaroos alive today.

6 ★★★ Think of three examples of natural environments in Exercise 1 that are in your country. What are their names?

______
______
______

GRAMMAR IN ACTION

The Second Conditional

1 ☆ **(Circle) the correct options.**

1 If I could travel anywhere in the world, …
  a I'll visit a jungle.
  (b) I'd visit a jungle.
  c I visited a jungle.

2 I don't know what would happen …
  a if all the insects will disappear.
  b if all the insects would disappear.
  c if all the insects disappeared.

3 What would happen if …
  a we cut down all the rainforests?
  b we'd cut down all the rainforests?
  c would we cut down all the rainforests?

4 If I were you, …
  a I'd find out more information.
  b I found out more information.
  c I'm finding out more information.

5 People wouldn't buy plastic products …
  a if they have a better alternative.
  b if they had a better alternative.
  c if they'd have a better alternative.

2 ☆☆ **Complete the second conditional sentences using the verbs in parentheses.**

1 If I ___had___ a bike, I ___would use___ it to go to school. (have / use)

2 I ________________ out today if it ________________ cold. (go / not be)

3 If they ________________ near the ocean, they ________________ to the beach a lot. (live / go)

4 The waterfall ________________ more interesting to look at if it ________________ raining. (be / be)

5 If we ________________ so much meat, we ________________ so many rainforests. (not eat / not cut down)

3 ☆☆ **Complete the blog post with the correct form of the verbs in the box to make second conditional sentences.**

be (x3)	~~can~~	check	find	not continue	not use	~~try~~

HOME | ABOUT ME | ARCHIVE | FOLLOW

If I [1] ___could___ do anything to help the planet, I [2] ___would try___ to stop people from buying so many things with palm oil in them. If you [3] ________________ the ingredients in the things you buy, you [4] ________________ palm oil in many of them – from cookies to toothpaste. It's a cheap type of oil, and our products [5] ________________ more expensive if companies [6] ________________ it.

The oil comes from trees that only grow in hot countries. This means that we need to cut down rainforests to grow them. This is a problem for the animals that live in rainforests, including the orangutan. If we [7] ________________ to destroy their natural habitat, orangutans wouldn't be endangered. So, if there [8] ________________ one useful thing everyone could do to protect the environment, it [9] ________________ to buy things that don't contain palm oil.

4 ☆☆ **Write second conditional questions and then write short answers (affirmative or negative).**

1 be so much waste / people not use so much plastic / ? (✗)
  Would ___there be so much waste if people didn't use so much plastic?___
  ___No, there wouldn't.___

2 we recycle more waste / help the environment / ? (✓)
  If ____
  ____

3 they use solar power / they have enough sunlight / ? (✓)
  Could ____
  ____

4 companies use palm oil / it not be cheap / ? (✗)
  Would ____
  ____

WRITING

An Opinion Essay

1 ☆ **Read the essay. Which environmental problem in the photos (a–c) does the writer think is the most serious?** ______

2 ☆☆ **Complete the essay with the words in the box. Sometimes more than one answer is possible.**

addition	~~believe~~	Furthermore	
However	opinion	summary	view

Our Most Serious Environmental Problem

There are many environmental problems nowadays, and it is difficult to know which one is the most important. Some people 1 ___believe___ that we should protect the rainforests. Other people might think that we need to stop using plastic. Which is the most important?

It would be good if we could solve both of these problems. 2 ______, in my 3 ______, the most serious problem is air pollution. This is something that is getting worse in cities around the world. 4 ______, it has an effect on everyone as it is a major cause of health problems, especially in children.

In my 5 ______, the first step would be to reduce the number of cars in cities. This is one of the biggest causes of pollution. In 6 ______, we need to make more people use public transportation or cleaner forms of personal transportation like bicycles. We also need cleaner factories that don't produce dangerous gases that are bad for our health.

In 7 ______, if we have cleaner cities with cleaner air, we will all become healthier. We will also spend more time outdoors, exercising and enjoying our natural environment.

3 ☆☆ **Circle the correct options.**

1. The first paragraph includes an introduction and *a question* / *the writer's main opinion*.
2. The second paragraph gives *the writer's main* / *other people's* opinion.
3. The third paragraph offers *reasons for* / *possible solutions to* the problem.
4. The last paragraph *introduces* / *summarizes* the writer's opinion.

a

b

c

PLAN

4 ☆☆ **Write your own opinion essay. Decide what you think is the biggest environmental problem and think of two possible solutions to the problem. Take notes.**

Problem: ______

Solution 1: ______

Solution 2: ______

5 **Decide what information to include in each paragraph. Use the information in Exercise 3 to help you.**

WRITE

6 ☆☆☆ **Write your opinion essay. Remember to include four paragraphs, the first and second conditional, and words and phrases from the *Useful Language* box (see Student's Book, p65).**

CHECK

7 **Do you ...**

- have an introduction with a question for the reader to think about?
- have solutions and examples to support your opinion?
- have a conclusion?

5 REVIEW

VOCABULARY

1 Match the beginnings of the sentences (1–10) with the ends (a–j).

1 Too much carbon ☐
2 It's important to save ☐
3 The biggest environmental problem is climate ☐
4 We all need to recycle and reduce waste to help protect the ☐
5 Plastic is a big problem for marine ☐
6 Plants produce ☐
7 The white rhino is ☐
8 We all live on the same ☐
9 Cars are the main cause of air ☐
10 Sunny countries produce a lot of energy from ☐

a change.
b an endangered species.
c oxygen, which all animals need to survive.
d planet, so we should take care of it.
e life, like fish, whales, and sea birds.
f dioxide causes global warming.
g pollution in cities.
h energy and not waste it.
i solar power.
j environment.

2 Match the sentences with the words in the box.

cave	cliff	coast	icebergs	rainforest	stream	volcano	waterfall

1 We walk here by the water as it flows through the forest. ________
2 My grandparents have a house there. It's nice because you can just walk out onto the beach and you can hear the ocean at night. ________
3 You can walk into it and it's really interesting. It's dark, but you can hear the sound of water deep below you. ________
4 Don't stand too close to the edge. I know it's nice to look down at the ocean, but it can be dangerous. ________
5 They cut down a large area. It will take hundreds of years for the trees and plants to grow again. ________
6 They're very dangerous to boats and ships. Remember that you can only see 10 percent of them. The rest is below the ocean. ________
7 Every second, almost 3 million liters of water drops to the river below at Niagara! ________
8 It's still active and you can often smell the gases – the heat and noise is incredible sometimes! ________

GRAMMAR IN ACTION

3 Mark (✓) the correct sentences and correct five incorrect sentences.

1 If I pass my exam tomorrow, I am really happy. ☐
____
2 I might go for a drive along the coast tomorrow if the weather will be nice. ☐
____
3 Will you call me if you're late? ☐
____
4 Unless I don't do my homework now, I won't have time to go out later. ☐
____
5 If I will have money, I will go to the movies on Friday. ☐
____
6 I won't buy a new phone unless this one breaks completely. ☐
____
7 If you look in the stream, you will may see some fish. ☐
____
8 You could take a break if you feel tired. ☐
____

4 Complete the sentences with the words in the box.

didn't have	had	knew	took	was	were	would be
would have	would need	would stop	would take	wouldn't be		

1 If I ______ time, I ______ a trip to the bay.
2 The town ______ in trouble if that volcano ______ active.
3 If you ______ more sociable, you ______ more friends.
4 You ______ sick if you ______ better care of yourself.
5 If I ______ a bike, I ______ to use the bus.
6 More people ______ eating meat if they ______ about the effects on the environment.

CUMULATIVE GRAMMAR

5 Complete the text with the missing words. Circle the correct options.

I [1] ______ a TV documentary last month about marine life and plastic. Every day, we [2] ______ a lot of plastic waste into the oceans, and even a little drinking straw can have a terrible effect on an animal. For example, if a fish [3] ______ one, it could easily die. And if a sea bird ate the fish, it [4] ______ the plastic, too. Plastic in the oceans is a big problem because it [5] ______ away. It just breaks down into smaller and smaller pieces! [6] ______ we do something about this problem, it will get worse. So, I [7] ______ to make some changes to my life. They're small, but if everyone [8] ______ something small, it would add up to something big. In the past, I [9] ______ a lot of plastic straws and bags. I [10] ______ straws without thinking about it in cafés. Now, I just say I don't need one when they offer. They haven't stopped using straws in cafés in my city [11] ______, but I hope they do soon. Anyway, we all need to do something. If we don't, then soon we [12] ______ to enjoy the natural beauty of the ocean and its marine life.

1	a have watched	b watched	c watch
2	a have put	b used to put	c put
3	a eats	b would eat	c will eat
4	a ate	b would eat	c will eat
5	a doesn't go	b wouldn't go	c isn't going
6	a If	b Furthermore	c Unless
7	a have decided	b am deciding	c will decide
8	a did	b does	c would do
9	a use to use	b used to use	c did use
10	a will use	b am using	c have used
11	a yet	b already	c since
12	a couldn't	b can't	c won't be able

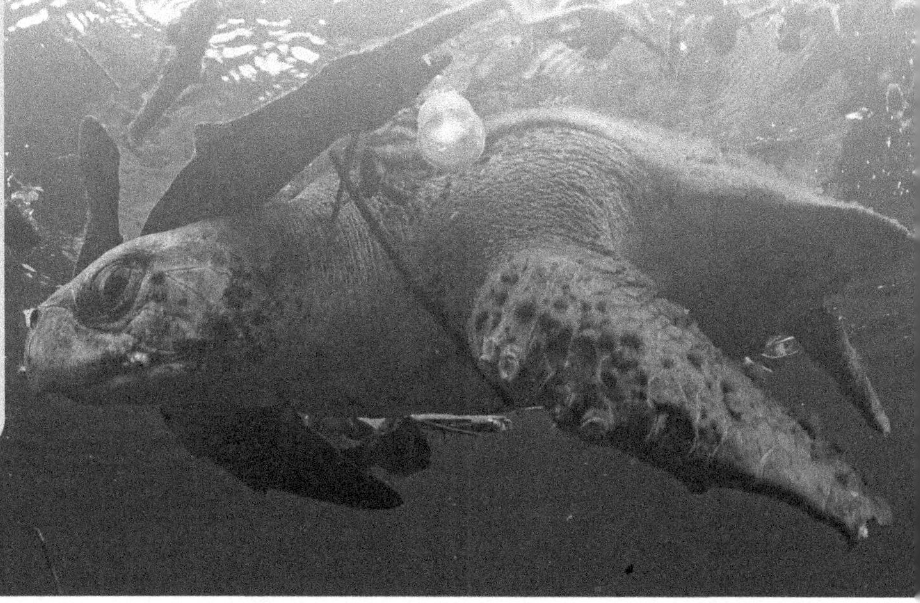

6 How can inventions change our lives?

VOCABULARY

Making Things

1 ☆ **Circle 12 more verbs in the word snake.**

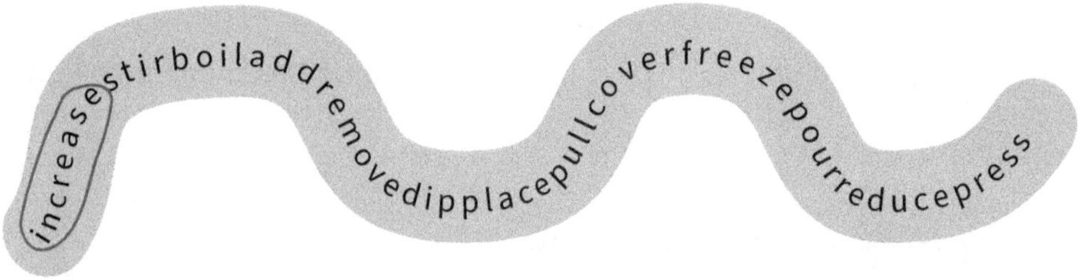

2 ☆☆ **Complete the sentences with the correct form of the verbs in Exercise 1.**

1. Increase the oven temperature from 150°C to 200°C.
2. I want to ________ the time I spend watching TV from four hours to one hour a day.
3. Water ________ at 100°C.
4. She ________ her feet in the ocean for a few seconds – it was really cold!
5. ________ the hot water into the cup and ________ sugar and milk.
6. ________ the cake from the oven and ________ it on a plate to cool.
7. You should ________ the soup with a spoon so it doesn't burn and stick to the pot.
8. I ________ my eyes so I couldn't see the frightening scenes in the movie.
9. Lara collects flowers – she ________ them flat and puts them in a scrapbook.
10. We use our car to ________ our camper when we go on vacation.
11. You should ________ fresh fish at –20°C for at least seven days before eating it.

3 ☆ **Choose one of the words in Exercise 1 and think of an image to go with it. Draw your image in your notebook (see the *Learn to Learn* tip in the Student's Book, p71).**

4 ☆☆ **Circle the correct words.**

1. When the milk boils, *pour* / *pull* it into your coffee cup.
2. *Reduce* / *Increase* the temperature so that it's really cold.
3. Take a spoon and *remove* / *stir* the butter, sugar, and milk together for a few minutes.
4. *Add* / *Cover* the glass with paper and put it in the fridge overnight.
5. I'll *freeze* / *press* any food that we don't eat, and we can have it next month.
6. Don't *dip* / *freeze* your finger into the hot liquid!

Explore It!

Guess the correct answer.

A chef in the U.S.A. invented chips when he …

a accidentally cooked some potatoes for too long.
b cut potatoes very thinly for an angry customer.
c poured hot fat over some frozen vegetables.

Find another interesting fact about an invention or discovery. Write a question and send it to a classmate in a text, or ask them in the next class.

READING

A News Story

1 ★★☆ **Read the news story. Complete the paragraphs (1–4) with the headings.**

What Was the Problem? What Do People Use It for Now?
What Was the Solution? Who Was Vesta Stoudt?

The Story of Duct Tape

1 ____________________

In the early 1940s, the U.S. army was fighting in Europe in World War II. Vesta Stoudt was a woman from Illinois who had two sons in the military. As part of the war effort, she was working in a factory in the U.S.A. Her job was to **inspect** and pack equipment for the soldiers in Europe.

2 ____________________

At the factory, they closed and **secured** the boxes of equipment using a thin paper **tape**. However, the boxes were difficult to open quickly, especially when they were wet. Vesta was worried that soldiers' lives might be in danger because they might not be able to get their equipment out fast enough.

3 ____________________

Vesta suggested that they close the boxes with a stronger, **waterproof** tape. She designed a basic **prototype** of how she thought the tape should be. The boxes were easier to open quickly with this new tape. Vesta's managers in the factory didn't listen to her, but she didn't give up. She decided to write to Franklin Roosevelt, the president of the United States.

4 ____________________

The letter worked and Vesta received a letter of thanks from Roosevelt. The government then asked a company to make the tape based on Vesta's idea. The tape was a great success and probably helped save lives! Nowadays, duct tape, as it is known, is used for many different things and in many different industries. It is used by NASA on its spaceships, and clothes are even made from it. And it's all thanks to the **patience** of one inspiring woman.

2 ★★☆ **Match the words in bold in the news story with the meanings.**

1 made safe from damage *secured*
2 stopping liquid from entering somewhere ____________
3 the ability to stay calm and continue doing something difficult ____________
4 view closely to check condition ____________
5 a long, narrow piece of material we use to close things ____________
6 the first example of something ____________

3 ★★☆ **Read the news story again and answer the questions.**

1 Where did Vesta Stoudt work?
She worked in a factory in the U.S.A.
2 What did Vesta do at the factory?
____
3 What problem did Vesta want to solve?
____
4 Why was Vesta's prototype better than the paper tape?
____
5 How did Vesta show patience?
____
6 What examples does the writer give of how people use duct tape now?
____

4 ★★★ **Can you think of any other ways people use duct tape? Write two ideas.**

____

GRAMMAR IN ACTION

Simple Present Passive

1 ★ **Complete the chart with the past participle form of the verbs. Mark if the verb is *R* (regular) or *I* (irregular).**

Verb	Past Participle	R	I
add	*added*	✓	
break			
catch			
collect			
connect			
design			
develop			
eat			
manufacture			
throw			

2 ★★ **Complete the sentences with the simple present passive form of the verbs in parentheses.**

1 How many smartphones *are made* every year in Asia? (make)

2 Something new and exciting ______ every day. (invent)

3 The potatoes ______ in very hot oil to make chips. (place)

4 These new inventions ______ enough, in my opinion. (not test)

5 ______ these materials ______ online or should we go to a store? (sell)

3 ★★ **Complete the sentences with the simple present passive form of verbs in Exercise 1.**

1 Food waste *is collected* for recycling.

2 Sugar ______ to chocolate to make it sweet.

3 How many plastic bottles ______ in the trash every day?

4 New ideas ______ here by brilliant young inventors.

5 ______ your computer ______ to the Internet by a cable or Wi-Fi?

6 This system ______ to help blind people use a computer.

4 ★★ **Write questions in the simple present passive. Then write the correct answers using the places in parentheses.**

1 coffee beans / grow / Iceland? (South America)

Are coffee beans grown in Iceland?

No, they aren't. Coffee beans are grown in South America.

2 most chocolate / produce / in Switzerland? (the U.S.A.)

______

______

3 these cars / manufacture / in Malta? (China)

______

______

4 insects / eat / in the UK? (Thailand)

______

______

5 bananas / grow / in Denmark? (Ecuador)

______

______

5 ★★★ **Complete the text with the simple present passive form of the verbs in parentheses.**

It's difficult to believe, but glass [1] *is made* (make) of liquid sand. That's right, the same sand that [2] ______ (find) on the beach or in the desert. When sand [3] ______ (heat) to about 1,700°C, it changes into a liquid. Other minerals[4] ______ (add), and when it cools to a much lower temperature, it changes into glass. To make glass containers, like jars and bottles, liquid glass [5] ______ (pour) into containers in a particular shape, called molds. Of course, glass [6] ______ also ______ (use) for windows, and we [7] ______ (protect) by glass, for example, in cars, but glass breaks easily, too. Glass [8] ______ easily ______ (recycle), so manufacturers can often use the same glass again and again in their products.

VOCABULARY AND LISTENING

Materials and Containers

1 ☆ **Match the materials with the containers in the box to make six objects. Then write the words in the correct column. Use each word only once.**

~~bag~~ box can cardboard case glass jar leather rubber ~~silk~~ tin tube

Material	Container
1 silk	bag
2	
3	
4	
5	
6	

2 ☆☆ **Complete the sentences with the objects in Exercise 1.**

1 Julia's dress doesn't have pockets. She needs a little silk bag to put her phone and wallet in.

2 A garden hose is a ________________. It's long and thin. You use it to water your flowers.

3 When Dad goes to work every morning, he carries his laptop and all his important papers in a ________________.

4 Our new computer came in a big ________________. We used it to put old books and clothes in.

5 Tuna, peas, and beans – what other things come in a ________________?

6 My grandma used to have a ________________ full of candy and chocolate for visiting children.

A Conversation

3 ☆ **Look at the questions and think about possible answers.**

1 What are jeans made of?
2 Who wears jeans?
3 How much do jeans cost?
4 What are the best styles?
5 What effect do jeans have on the environment?

6.01 **4** ☆ **Listen to two friends shopping for jeans. Which three questions in Exercise 3 do the girls discuss?**

____

6.01 **5** ☆☆ **Listen again. Are the sentences *T* (true) or *F* (false)? Correct the false sentences.**

1 Nicole prefers white jeans to blue jeans. F
Nicole prefers blue jeans.

2 The word "denim" comes from the name of a French town. ___
____

3 Camila says good jeans can cost about $100. ___
____

4 Nicole says that some jeans factories use too much energy. ___
____

5 Nicole says Camila should find out information before she buys jeans. ___
____

6 Camila doesn't want to go to the store that Nicole suggests. ___
____

GRAMMAR IN ACTION

Simple Past Passive

1 ★ **Complete the sentences with the simple past passive form of the verbs in parentheses.**

1 Tolstoy's novel *War and Peace* ___was___ ___published___ (publish) in 1867.

2 The world's most expensive violins __________ (make) by Antonio Stradivari.

3 Facebook __________ (start) by Harvard University students in 2004.

4 Is it true that some of Shakespeare's plays __________ (not write) by him?

5 A lot of my photos __________ (lose) when my phone broke.

6 Paper __________ (not invent) in Europe but in China.

2 ★★ **Write questions in the simple past passive.**

1 when / first antibiotic / discover?
___When was the first antibiotic discovered?___

2 where / the world's first subway / open?
____

3 where / the first modern Olympics / hold?
____

4 what / the first Pixar movie / call?
____

5 where / the largest Egyptian pyramids / build?
____

6 when / the first email / write?
____

7 where / the first CD / make?
____

8 when / Google / start?
____

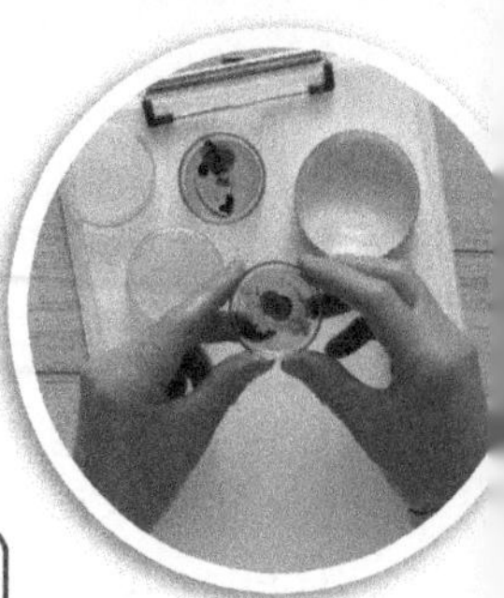

3 ★★ **Match the answers in the box with the questions in Exercise 2. Check your answers on the Internet if necessary. Then write sentences in the simple past passive.**

~~1928~~	1971	1998	Athens	Germany
Giza	London	*Toy Story*		

1 ___The first antibiotic was discovered in 1928.___
2 __________
3 __________
4 __________
5 __________
6 __________
7 __________
8 __________

4 ★★★ **Read the text about Stonehenge. Rewrite the underlined phrases using the simple past passive.**

Who built Stonehenge and why [1]<u>someone built it</u> continues to be a great mystery. It is one of the most famous prehistoric monuments in the UK. [2]<u>Someone started the building of Stonehenge</u> about 5,000 years ago. Some people believe that [3]<u>someone used Stonehenge</u> in a celebration of the sun. [4]<u>Someone designed it</u> in exact mathematical detail, as the stone circle perfectly matches the direction of the midsummer sunrise and the midwinter sunset. There are two types of stone at Stonehenge. The larger stones are called "sarsens." The tallest sarsen stands nine meters high and weighs 25 tons – [5]<u>someone carried the stones</u> 32 kilometers to Stonehenge! The smaller "bluestones" weigh much less, but [6]<u>someone brought these stones</u> from Wales, a distance of 225 kilometers. Nobody knows how [7]<u>someone transported such heavy stones</u> so far in those days.

1 ___it was built___
2 __________
3 __________
4 __________
5 __________
6 __________
7 __________

WRITING

A Review

1 ★ **Look at the photo and read the review. Is everything about the smartwatch positive?**

____

1 If you're serious about your fitness training, you'll find this smartwatch very helpful. It counts the calories used in every activity you do. It also gives information on goals, such as distance and speed, and tells you your heart rate. You can connect it to your favorite fitness apps so that your performance can help improve your training.

2 This smartwatch is light and comfortable. The strap looks like silk, though it's actually made from soft rubber. It looks cool and modern, and it feels like silk on your skin, too, so you won't know you're wearing it! It's also waterproof, so you can walk straight into the shower after your workout. The battery life is very good: it lasts up to 20 hours and it recharges very quickly.

3 What I like about this smartwatch is that it's sporty and strong, but it's also really comfortable, so you can wear it all day. However, I should point out that it's not cheap. Overall, I think it's a really cool invention and I'm really happy I bought this model!

2 ★★ **Read the review again. In which paragraph (1–3) can you find …**

a a description of what the invention does? [1]

b what the reviewer likes the most? [ ]

c a physical description? [ ]

d the reviewer's general opinion? [ ]

e a disadvantage? [ ]

f who the invention is for? [ ]

3 ★★ **Put the words in the correct order to make the *Useful Language* phrases.**

1 made from / soft rubber / is / The strap

The strap is made from soft rubber.

2 it's a / really cool invention / Overall, / I think

____

3 it's sporty and strong / about this smartwatch / is that / What I like

____

4 it's not cheap / point out that / I should / However,

____

5 The strap / looks / silk / like

____

PLAN

4 ★★ **Write your own review. Choose an amazing digital device or gadget and take notes.**

Who the device or gadget is for: ______________________________

What it does: ______________________________

What it looks like: ______________________________

The advantages: ______________________________

One disadvantage: ______________________________

Your opinion: ______________________________

WRITE

5 ★★★ **Write your review. Remember to include the parts of the review from Exercise 2, the passive, and phrases from the *Useful Language* box (see Student's Book, p77).**

CHECK

6 **Do you …**

- describe what the device/gadget does and who it's for?
- give a physical description?
- say what the advantages/disadvantages are?
- give your general opinion?

6 REVIEW

VOCABULARY

1 Match the beginnings of the sentences (1–8) with the ends (a–h).

1 If the fruit has pits in it, ☐
2 You should reduce the ☐
3 Don't dip your fingers into ☐
4 Palm oil boils ☐
5 Add the sugar to the water ☐
6 We waited for the liquid to freeze ☐
7 Carefully pour the liquid ☐
8 Pull the paper off the ☐

a temperature when the sauce gets too hot.
b at about 300°C.
c solid before we ate the ice pops.
d and stir both of them together.
e into the molds.
f remove them before you cook it.
g ice pops before the children eat them.
h very hot water – it's dangerous!

2 Underline and correct one mistake with materials and containers in each sentence.

1 The clothes and shoes were packed in cardboard jars. ________
2 It's better to use glass boxes for jam so you can recycle them. ________
3 We gave our mom a pretty silk tube for her birthday. ________
4 We don't know what is in this tin bag because there's no label. ________
5 Our teacher always carries our homework and exam papers in a leather can. ________
6 Hospitals have a lot of rubber cases for medical use. ________

GRAMMAR IN ACTION

3 Complete the conversation with the simple present passive form of the verbs in parentheses.

RYAN Do you know how much coffee [1] ________ (make) every year?

HARI I'm sure it's a lot. I know that loads of coffee [2] ________ (use) in my house!

RYAN Well, they estimate that over two billion cups of coffee [3] ________ (drink) worldwide every day.

HARI Wow! That is amazing! And where [4] ________ all that coffee ________ (grow)? South America?

RYAN Yes, well, most of the coffee that [5] ________ (buy) in the U.S.A. [6] ________ (produce) in Brazil.

HARI I guess the climate is just right there.

RYAN Yes, it's perfect because coffee [7] ________ (plant) in the wet season, but sunshine [8] ________ (need) later in the process. The coffee beans [9] ________ (dry) in the sun and [10] ________ (test) by experts.

HARI Hmm, how about a cup right now?

RYAN Good idea!

4 Put the words in the correct order to make simple past passive questions. Then write answers using the words in parentheses.

1 was / When / the / build / Taj Mahal / ? (around 1640)

____

____

2 open / was / this / When / middle school / ? (in 2010)

____

____

3 were / Where / these / make / computers / ? (in Japan)

____

____

4 cave paintings / were / those / Where / old / find / ? (in France)

____

____

5 was / Where / tea / grow / first / ? (in China)

____

____

6 write / was / When / *Macbeth* / ? (in 1606)

____

____

CUMULATIVE GRAMMAR

5 Complete the text with the missing words. Circle the correct options.

I [1]_____ an interesting article about important inventions the other day. [2]_____ that plastic shopping bags [3]_____ in the 1960s by a Swedish engineer? Before plastic was invented, shoppers [4]_____ paper bags. These were much better for the environment. Nowadays, governments [5]_____ to find ways to reduce the use of plastic bags. Ideas include "Bags for Life." These bags [6]_____ of cotton and are very strong, so shoppers can use them again and again. Supermarkets have also [7]_____ charging customers for their plastic bags. The article also said that scientists believe they [8]_____ a special bacteria that [9]_____ eat plastic. The bacteria was discovered in a Japanese recycling center in 2016. While the scientists [10]_____ the bacteria, they accidentally made it even better at eating plastic! At the moment, the bacteria can only eat the plastic in drink bottles, but in the future, it [11]_____ be able to eat all types of plastic! If scientists [12]_____ a super bacteria to eat all plastic, plastic bags would become a thing of the past!

	a	b	c
1	read	have read	did read
2	Were you knowing	Did you knew	Did you know
3	was invented	were invented	invented
4	used to use	use to use	use to using
5	try	tried	are trying
6	are made	is made	made
7	begin	begun	began
8	invented	are invented	have invented
9	can	can to	can will
10	investigated	have investigated	were investigating
11	might	can	may not
12	would create	could create	might create

7 What do you celebrate?

1 a *fair* / *parade*

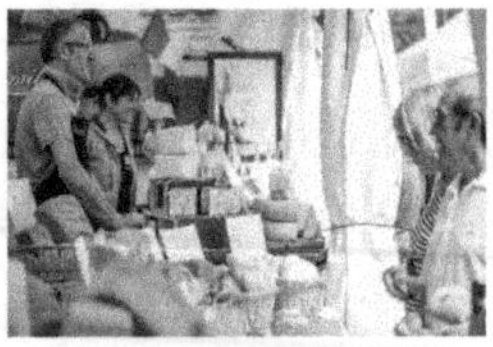

2 *an atmosphere* / *a stall*

VOCABULARY

Festivals

1 ★ Look at the photos and circle the correct options.

3 *a costume* / *decoration*

4 *a parade* / *float*

5 *a lantern* / *fireworks*

2 ★★ Complete the article with the correct form of words in Exercise 1.

6 *decorations* / *a float*

7 *a program* / *fair*

8 *a parade* / *program*

9 *fireworks* / *a lantern*

Celebrations Around the World

One of the biggest festivals in Japan is the Gion Festival in Narita, a small town near Tokyo. It's a celebration of the summer. There are colorful 1 decorations all over the town, and people dress up in traditional Japanese 2 ________ . Visitors can enjoy food and drinks at the many 3 ________ in Narita's narrow streets. The best part of the festival is when decorated 4 ________ with people on them are pulled through the streets to Narita's main temple. The streets of Narita are beautiful at night when they are lit up by 5 ________ on the sides of the buildings.

New Year's Eve is always special in Sydney, Australia. You can see a beautiful display of 6 ________ in the night sky, with thousands exploding over the Sydney Opera House. There are a lot of things to do during the day, too. Children can enjoy fantastic rides at the 7 ________ , like a 40-meter Ferris wheel or a super-fast train. In the evening, people love the 8 ________ of boats traveling up and down the harbor with special lights on them!

3 ★★ Circle the correct options.

1 There was already *a crowd* / *an atmosphere* of 50,000 people at ten o'clock!

2 The band marched in the *ceremony* / *parade* down Main Street.

3 Great music and a lot of people usually make a good *program* / *atmosphere*.

4 A *fair* / *ceremony* is usually a formal event with a long history.

4 ★★ Underline the stressed syllable in each word.

Two Syllables	Three Syllables	Four Syllables
costume	atmosphere	ceremony
fireworks		decoration
lantern		
parade		

Explore It!

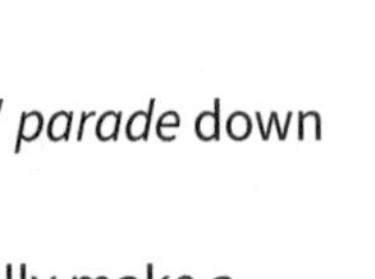

Guess the correct answer.

The famous Japanese … ceremony began around 700 years ago.

a tea b coffee c milk

Find another interesting fact about an ancient ceremony. Write a question and send it to a classmate in an email, or ask them in the next class.

READING

A Folktale

1 **Look at the pictures. What do you think the folktale is about? Read the story and (circle) the correct answer.**

a a prince who lost his son

b a very brave dog

c a brave prince who killed a wolf

2 **Match the words in bold in the folktale with the meanings.**

1 very shocked ___horrified___

2 a long piece of metal used for fighting ______

3 chasing and trying to catch and kill an animal ______

4 a place in the ground where a dead body is put ______

5 strong and not changing in your friendship with someone ______

6 put something into a hole in the ground and covered it ______

3 **Read the folktale again. (Circle) the correct answers.**

1 Why did the prince have dogs?

a because he was lonely

b to take care of his castle

(c) to look for other animals

2 What did the prince think when he saw blood on his dog?

a His son was hurt.

b Something was missing.

c The dog was hurt.

3 What did the dog do?

a He killed the prince's son.

b He killed a dangerous animal.

c He hid behind a bed.

4 What happened at the end?

a Everyone forgot about the dog.

b The village was given the dog's name.

c The prince found another dog.

The Wolf and a Baby Boy

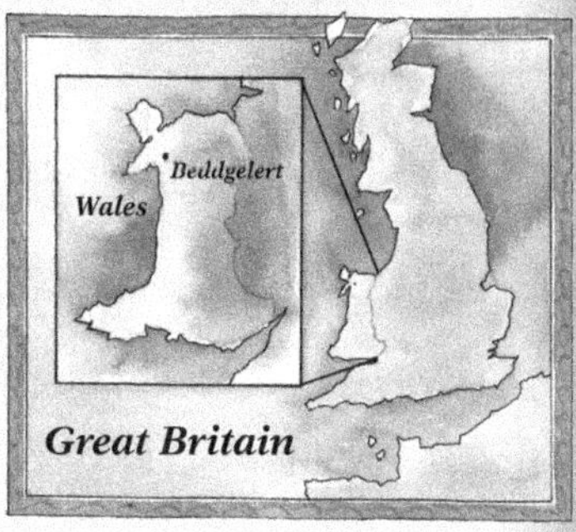

In the north of Wales, there is a small village named Beddgelert. According to an old story, many hundreds of years ago, a prince lived in the area. It was a place of forests and dangerous wild animals. The prince loved **hunting**, so he had many dogs. They spent a lot of time chasing animals through the forests for sport. His favorite dog was named Gelert – a **faithful** dog who the prince loved.

One day, the prince decided to go hunting and called for Gelert. To the prince's surprise, the dog came with blood around its mouth. The prince was **horrified**. Where had the blood come from? He had a terrible thought. He ran to his son's bedroom and saw an awful sight. His baby was missing and the floor was covered in blood. The prince realized what the dog had done. With anger, he took a **sword** and killed Gelert. Seconds later, the prince heard a cry from behind the bed. There was his son, completely safe. And next to his son was a wolf – killed by Gelert, just a few minutes earlier. The prince felt very sad. He carried his favorite dog outside and **buried** it under some stones.

Beddgelert means "Gelert's grave" in the Welsh language, and you can see stones marking the **grave** in the village. However, the story might not be true. Some people say that a hotel owner placed the stones there 200 years ago and, perhaps, invented the story to bring in more tourists. And it worked! Now there are many events in the town, from music festivals to fireworks displays on New Year's Eve. In the summer, people in the town grow lots of flowers as decorations, and Beddgelert has won competitions for being the most beautiful town in the country!

4 **Think of a folktale from your country. Write a paragraph about it in your notebook.**

GRAMMAR IN ACTION

Past Perfect

1 ★ **Match sentences 1–6 with a–f.**

1 I felt very tired. [f]
2 I couldn't go to the concert. [ ]
3 I already knew the story of the movie. [ ]
4 I said I was sorry for being late. [ ]
5 I got lost when I went to Quito. [ ]
6 I didn't know what time the concert started. [ ]

a I hadn't looked at the program.
b I hadn't bought any tickets.
c I had read the book.
d I hadn't finished my work on time.
e I hadn't been there before.
f I hadn't slept enough.

2 ★★ **Read the sentences. Circle the action that happened first, *A* or *B*.**

1 She went to see the fireworks because her friends had invited her.
A She went to see the fireworks.
(B) Her friends invited her.

2 When I saw the program, I knew I'd seen the show before.
A I saw the program.
B I saw the show.

3 They'd arranged to meet at the food stall, but Tom couldn't find Katy.
A They arranged to meet.
B Tom couldn't find Katy.

4 After he'd called his mom, he ordered a pizza.
A He ordered a pizza.
B He called his mom.

5 Megan felt a little upset after she'd said goodbye to them.
A Megan said goodbye to them.
B She felt a little upset.

3 ★★ **Complete the sentences with the past perfect form of the verbs in parentheses.**

1 I hadn't bought (not buy) a costume, so I didn't have anything special to wear to the parade.
2 Talia ________ (not hear) of the festival before she went there.
3 He got to the concert 20 minutes after it ________ (start).
4 They went to Miami last year, and they were also there 30 years ago. It ________ (change) a lot.
5 We didn't want to see the new *Bond* movie because we ________ (not see) the previous one yet.
6 When I got home, I realized that I ________ (leave) my phone at school.

4 ★★ **Circle the correct options.**

PAULA [1] *(Did you go)* / *Had you been* anywhere interesting for your vacation?

MARCO Well, I [2] *visited* / *had visited* my grandparents in northern Italy in September. They took me to a town named Marostica. I [3] *didn't go* / *hadn't been* there before.

PAULA Was it nice?

MARCO Yes, they have a chess festival there.

PAULA Chess festival? That doesn't sound very interesting!

MARCO But it was! My grandparents [4] *told* / *had told* me a lot about it before I [5] *went* / *had been*, and I'd thought the same as you. But there was a giant chess set in the middle of the town! And people were dressed in costumes as chess pieces, and they [6] *moved* / *had moved* around the board.

PAULA Oh, do they do that every year?

MARCO Every two years. It's to celebrate a famous chess match that two princes [7] *played* / *had played* about 600 years ago. They [8] *fell* / *had fallen* in love with the same woman, but instead of fighting, they decided to play chess!

VOCABULARY AND LISTENING

Music Festivals and Live Music

1 ☆ **Complete the lists with the words in the box. One word can go in more than one list.**

~~band member~~ campsite encore gig headliner stage supporting act tent track venue

1 where you can see a band: ________ ________ ________

2 where you can stay the night: ________ ________

3 singers or musicians: band member ________ ________ ________

4 ways to hear a song ________ ________ ________

2 ☆☆ **Complete the text with the correct form of words in Exercise 1.**

The 1 venue for the Coachella Festival is a polo club in California. Thousands of music fans go there to see their favorite bands. 2 ________ at Coachella have included some of the biggest names in music, like Radiohead and Beyoncé. There are also lots of interesting, less famous 3 ________ to see. These bands play on smaller 4 ________ in front of smaller crowds. Visitors to the festival can stay at a big 5 ________ with a lot of 6 ________. There's always a great atmosphere at Coachella, and the bands always leave the fans shouting for an 7 ________.

A Conversation

7.01 **3** ☆ **Listen to the conversation. What is unusual about the Secret Solstice Festival?**

____

7.01 **4** ☆☆ **Listen again. Are the sentences *T* (true) or *F* (false)?**

1 Antonio hasn't been to the Secret Solstice Festival. T

2 The weather isn't very cold at the festival. ____

3 Famous bands don't play at the festival. ____

4 One of the venues is in a dangerous place. ____

5 Antonio's brother didn't have a ticket for the volcano gig. ____

5 ☆☆ **Look at Exercise 6. What type of information (object, number, or place) is missing in 1–7? (See the *Learn to Learn* tip in the Student's Book, page 86).**

____

7.01 **6** ☆☆☆ **Complete the summary about the Secret Solstice festival. Then listen again and check.**

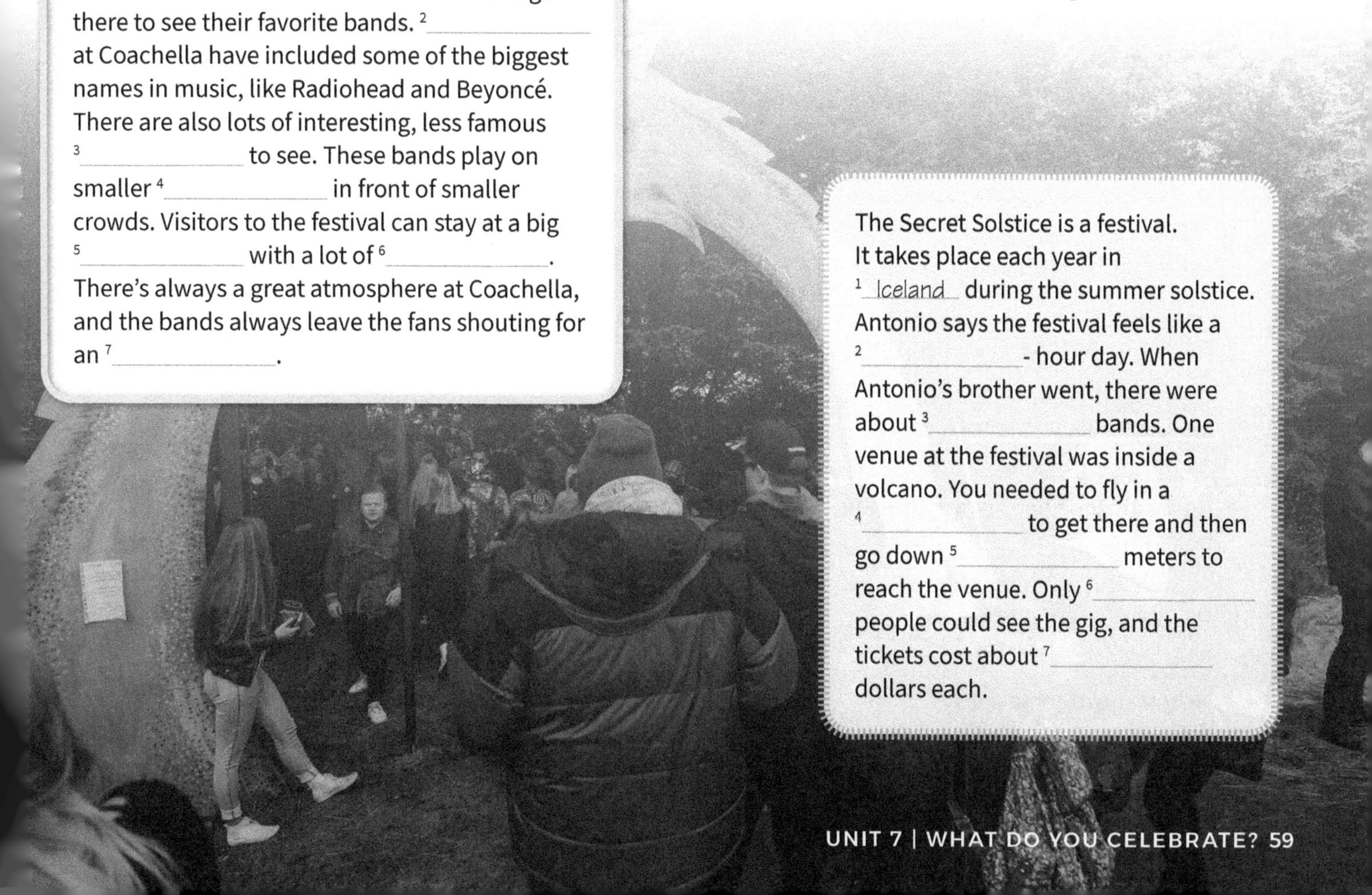

The Secret Solstice is a festival. It takes place each year in 1 Iceland during the summer solstice. Antonio says the festival feels like a 2 ________ - hour day. When Antonio's brother went, there were about 3 ________ bands. One venue at the festival was inside a volcano. You needed to fly in a 4 ________ to get there and then go down 5 ________ meters to reach the venue. Only 6 ________ people could see the gig, and the tickets cost about 7 ________ dollars each.

GRAMMAR IN ACTION

Reported Statements

1 ★ How do the tenses and verbs change in reported speech? Complete the table.

Direct Speech	Reported Speech
Simple Present	1 Simple Past
Simple Past	2
Present Perfect	3
Present Continuous	4
Will	5
Can	6

2 ★ Complete the sentences with *said* or *told*.

1 My sister ___said___ she went to a really interesting music festival last year.

2 George ___________ me that he had some new tracks for me to listen to.

3 I ___________ everyone that I had a spare ticket for the concert.

4 Sally ___________ that she couldn't go to the campsite because she didn't have a tent.

5 Laura ___________ us to meet her in front of the stage.

6 I ___________ I didn't know who the supporting act was.

3 ★★ Rewrite the reported speech as direct speech.

1 Ashraf said that he was in a café.
"I'm in a café. ___________"

2 He told me that he was having lunch.
"___________"

3 He said he wanted to meet me.
"___________"

4 He said that he had been in the café for an hour.
"___________"

5 He told me he would leave in about 30 minutes.
"___________"

6 He told me to come quickly.
"___________"

4 ★★ Read the conversation. Then complete the reported speech below.

ME Hi, Dan!
DAN Hi! I'm really happy to see you! I have some exciting news. I'm thinking of going to a festival in the summer. I want you to come with me.
ME Hmm, I'm not sure. Where is it? How much is it?
DAN It's not far away. It's in the country. The tickets are about $30. I've been there before. I had a great time.
ME OK, but where would we stay?
DAN Well, there's a campsite. We can stay in a tent. It won't be expensive.
ME OK, I'll think about it.
DAN Great!

I went to the café to meet Dan. He said that he [1] ___was___ happy to see me and that he [2] ___________ some exciting news. He told me that he [3] ___________ of going to a festival in the summer, and then he told me that he [4] ___________ me to go with him. I said that I [5] ___________ sure, and I asked where the festival was and how much it was. Ashraf said that it [6] ___________ far away, in the country, and the tickets [7] ___________ about $30. He said that he [8] ___________ there before and that he [9] ___________ a great time. He also said that we [10] ___________ in a tent, so it [11] ___________ very expensive. I said that I [12] ___________ about it.

5 ★★★ Think of a conversation you had with someone recently. What did you talk about? Write at least five sentences using reported speech.

I was talking to Mom yesterday. She told me … ___________

____

____

____

____

____

WRITING

An Email to a Friend

1 ★ **Read the email quickly. (Circle) the photo that matches it.**

a

b

c

Home Inbox Sent New

From: Karen

To: Matt

Hello Matt,

[1]<u>I just got your message, thanks.</u> [2]<u>It was nice of you to write!</u>

You said you wanted to know all about the festival. I'd never been to anything like it before, but it was great! I only spent a day there, but I saw so many amazing things. There were a lot of people dressed as characters from movies and TV. I'm attaching a photo of some people I met. They live near you! They told me to say hello to you! I think I was the only one not wearing a costume! I felt strange walking around in normal clothes!

In the afternoon, there was an event with some really famous actors from *Star Wars*. There were probably around 500 people in the audience, asking questions. Unfortunately, I didn't get the chance to ask anything. But one of the guests said that she had just filmed something really exciting for the next movie. Then she told us! I can't say anything – it's a spoiler!

OK, [3]<u>I have to go now.</u> [4]<u>I hope to hear from you soon.</u>

[5]<u>I'll be in touch later,</u>

Karen

2 ★★ **Put a–e in the order they appear in the email (1–5).**

a ☐ request for a reply
b ☐ goodbye
c ☐ description of the festival
d [1] greeting
e ☐ thanks for writing

3 ★★ **Match the <u>underlined</u> phrases in the email (1–5) with the *Useful Language* phrases (a–e).**

a Write back soon. [4]
b Anyway, that's all from me. ☐
c Bye for now. ☐
d It was great to hear from you. ☐
e Thanks for your email. ☐

PLAN

4 ★★ **Write your own email about a festival you have been to. Take notes.**

What kind of festival was it? ______

What did people wear? ______

What did people do? ______

What did you see and do? ______

How did you feel? ______

5 **Decide what information to include. Use the structure in Exercise 2 to help you.**

WRITE

6 ★★★ **Write your email. Remember to include the past perfect, reported speech, and phrases from the *Useful Language* box (see Student's Book, p89).**

CHECK

7 **Do you ...**

- have a greeting and a goodbye?
- describe the festival?
- request a reply?

7 REVIEW

VOCABULARY

1 Match the definitions with the words in the box.

costume decoration fair fireworks float lantern parade program stall

1 something you use to make things look more interesting or beautiful ______
2 a plan of all the activities and events at a festival ______
3 a big table on the street where people can buy things ______
4 a big decorated truck that moves through the streets at festivals ______
5 a light that people can hold or hang up in public places ______
6 the clothes you wear for a special activity ______
7 something that makes beautiful lights and noises in the night sky ______
8 a large number of people walking together, usually to celebrate something ______
9 a place with games and machines you can ride on ______

2 Complete the sentences with words for live music and festivals.

1 There were three b______ m______ in Clean Bandit: Grace Chatto, and Jack and Luke Patterson.
2 At the end of the concert, the audience shouted for more, and the band came back for an e______.
3 It was a terrible v______ for a concert. I couldn't see the stage because it was really far away.
4 I don't think this year's festival will be very good. The h______ is a band from the 1990s that no one has heard of.
5 We went to a small g______ last night – it was one of the best live events I've been to.
6 Did you know that there is a bonus t______ at the end of the album? Most people don't know about it.
7 Sometimes, the s______ a______ is better than the main performer.
8 The festival has a big c______ with space for nearly 500 tents.

GRAMMAR IN ACTION

3 Complete the sentences with the past perfect form of the verbs in the box.

be buy decorate hear not see sell

1 I didn't go to the festival because I ______ that it was going to rain.
2 I'm glad that we ______ the tickets early because they became really expensive later.
3 By the time the headliners appeared, the supporting acts ______ on stage for an hour.
4 My sister loved the concert. She ______ anything like it before.
5 When you checked the tickets online, ______ they ______ them all?
6 People ______ the street with lanterns and it looked beautiful.

4 **What did Mike say? Change the direct speech into reported speech.**

1 "I want to go home."

Mike said that ________________.

2 "I don't feel well."

Mike said that ________________.

3 "I've taken some medicine."

Mike said that ________________.

4 "I'll take a taxi home."

Mike said that ________________.

5 "I can't find a taxi number!"

Mike said that ________________.

6 "I'll ask my mom to come get me."

Mike said that ________________.

CUMULATIVE GRAMMAR

5 **Complete the text with the missing words. Circle the correct options.**

I live in a small town. It's nice, but nothing interesting ever [1]_____ . So I was really surprised when my dad [2]_____ me that there would be a big celebration. He said that the bridge in the town [3]_____ 200 years old this summer, and there would be a huge party. At first, I said that I wasn't interested. I [4]_____ over that bridge thousands of times going to school and I [5]_____ see it during my summer vacation. But then my dad said, "If you [6]_____ to the festival, you'll have a great time." So I went. And it really was great! Everyone was dressed up in costumes, and they had a parade through the center of town. The whole town [7]_____ like a big history lesson! And in the evening, there [8]_____ a big fireworks display. Earlier that day, I [9]_____ that the bridge was really important in history. It [10]_____ by a famous architect. I [11]_____ it was just a boring bridge! It was a great day, but I still don't think there are [12]_____ in my town!

1	a happens	b had happened	c is happening
2	a said	b asked	c told
3	a is being	b would be	c should be
4	a have been	b had	c was
5	a not want	b didn't want to	c didn't wanted
6	a come	b will come	c came
7	a looks	b looking	c looked
8	a was	b were	c had been
9	a was learning	b had learned	c have learned
10	a is built	b built	c was built
11	a was thinking	b used to think	c don't think
12	a festivals enough	b too festivals	c enough festivals

8 What is education?

VOCABULARY

School

1 ★ Circle the correct verbs to complete the phrases about school.

1 *cheat* / *pay* on a test
2 *tell* / *fail* an exam
3 *get* / *pay* detention
4 *study* / *get* good grades
5 *pay* / *give* (somebody) a talk
6 *hand* / *pass* in homework
7 *cheat* / *pass* an exam
8 *pay* / *get* attention to the teacher
9 *study* / *take* for a test
10 *take* / *pay* an exam
11 *write* / *study* an essay

2 ★ Look at phrases 1–8 in Exercise 1. Write them in the correct column.

Positive Things	Negative Things
______	cheat on a test
______	______
______	______
______	______

3 ★★ Complete the sentences with the correct form of phrases in Exercise 1.

1 I took an exam last week, but I'm not sure how well I did.
2 If you ______ for bad behavior, you won't be able to go to basketball practice after school!
3 He doesn't always ______ on his schoolwork – last week he got a D on an essay.
4 Tania was very pleased when she ______ all her ______ – she got As in history and science!
5 I can't go out tonight. I need to ______ on capital cities, and I haven't learned them all yet.
6 I ______ on ancient history – I got an F! I need to take it again.
7 Why did the teacher ______ you ______? What did you do to make him angry?
8 Please try to ______ on time, Sam! That's the second time you've given it to me late this week!
9 Someone ______ in Ms. Clarke's class. They used their phone to look up the answers!
10 Unless you ______ and listen to everything he says, you won't know how to do the project.

4 ★★★ Complete the sentences so they are true for you.

1 If I saw someone cheating on a test, I would ______.
2 It's important for me to get good grades because ______.
3 The last time I failed an exam was ______.
4 One important exam I will take this year is ______.
5 I usually study for tests ______.

Explore It!

Guess the correct answer.

The highest school in the world is called Phumachangtang in the Himalayas. The school is more than ... meters above sea level.

a 4,000 b 5,000 c 6,000

Find an interesting fact about education in your country. Write a question and send it to a classmate in an email, or ask them in the next class.

READING
A Report

1 ☆ **What do you think is happening in the photo? Read the report and check your ideas.**

____

SCHOOL'S OUT

More than a million people are homeschooled in the U.S.A. **Reasons** for homeschooling can include a child's special needs, **bullying**, or **a lack of** good school options in the area. We spoke to one "homeschooler," Andrew James, from Atlanta, Georgia, about his experiences of homeschooling.

"I started homeschooling three years ago – I'm 14 now. When I left elementary school, I went straight to homeschooling, so I've never been to middle school. My mom was also homeschooled, so she was **into** us having a similar education to hers. My parents believe that education is not just about getting good grades or taking exams – they think a **balanced** education, including practical skills, is also important.

My younger brother and I study at home with our parents for seven hours a day. Both our parents used to be teachers – so that helps! But having school at home doesn't mean there aren't any rules. We're not allowed to stay in bed all day, obviously, but we can also choose what we learn. Of course, we study normal subjects, but we also frequently go to libraries, museums, exhibitions, concerts, and sporting events as part of our education.

We can also do other things that maybe you can't do at an ordinary school. For example, each year my brother and I are allowed to plan a big trip to a place connected to something we are studying. My brother studies geology, so we went to Mount Vesuvius in Italy to learn about volcanoes. Next year, I want to go to Amsterdam to visit the house of Anne Frank because I'm learning about her famous **diary** in my history lessons.

It's not all vacations and day trips – we work really hard and study a lot! But I really love my home education. I wouldn't change it for anything!"

2 ☆☆ **Match the words in bold in the report with the meanings.**

1 having equal amounts of something *balanced*
2 a book with someone's thoughts and feelings ______
3 the causes of an event or situation ______
4 very interested in ______
5 not enough of something ______
6 when someone hurts or frightens someone else ______

3 ☆☆ **Read the report again. Are the sentences *T* (true) or *F* (false)? Correct the false sentences.**

1 Andrew has never attended an ordinary school.
F. He went to an ordinary elementary school.
2 Andrew started homeschooling because his mom didn't like his school.
______
3 His parents taught at schools before they homeschooled Andrew.
______
4 Andrew and his brother do some studying outside their home.
______
5 Their trips to other places are part of their education.
______
6 Andrew would like to go back to ordinary school in the future.
______

4 ☆☆☆ **Think of two possible disadvantages of homeschooling.**

______
______

GRAMMAR IN ACTION

Can/Can't

1 ★ What do the sentences express? Write *permission*, *prohibition*, or *ability*.

1 Marcus can't leave yet because he has detention. ______

2 You got a very good grade on your essay. Can I read it? ______

3 Sonia can play two instruments, and she's a great singer, too. ______

2 ★ (Circle) the correct options.

1 In my school, we (*can*) / *can't* learn Latin if we want.

2 My sister *can* / *can't* speak Italian, but she speaks German well.

3 Mrs. Evans says I *can* / *can't* leave until I've finished this exercise.

4 *Can* / *Can't* I borrow your dictionary, please?

5 We *can* / *can't* understand you when you speak clearly.

6 You *can* / *can't* stay in bed all day. It's bad for you.

To Be Allowed To

3 ★★ Put the words in the correct order to make sentences. Then mark (✓) the sentences that are true for your school.

1 school / at / wear / allowed / Students / aren't / jewelery / to ☐

Students aren't allowed to wear jewelery at school.

2 lunchtime / allowed / phones / We / at / use / to / are / our ☐

______

3 break time / soccer / play / Students / at / are / allowed / to ☐

______

4 shout / allowed / aren't / the / You / teachers / to / at ☐

______

4 ★★ Write questions and short answers with the correct form of *to be allowed to*.

1 you / cycle to school? (yes)

Are you allowed to cycle to school? Yes, I am.

2 your teachers / give detention? (yes)

______

3 students / wear any clothes they like? (no)

______

4 students / talk during exams? (no)

______

5 your best friend / sit next to you? (yes)

______

6 your parents / help with homework? (no)

______

5 ★★ Complete the text with the missing words. (Circle) the correct options.

I think it's hard to be the youngest in the family. My big sister [1] ______ to go to bed when she wants, but I [2] ______. On Fridays and Saturdays, I [3] ______ stay up later, but not as late as my sister. And my big brothers [4] ______ watch late shows on TV! But they [5] ______ to leave the house without helping our parents. They [6] ______ go to college by car, but I [7] ______ drive yet, so I cycle to school. All the people in my family [8] ______ give me a talk because I'm the youngest – it's so unfair!

	a	b	c
1	(a) is allowed	b are allowed	c can
2	a can	b 'm not	c isn't
3	a can't	b can	c 'm not allowed to
4	a can to	b is allowed to	c are allowed to
5	a aren't allowed	b can't	c not allowed
6	a can	b can't	c aren't allowed to
7	a 'm allowed to	b can	c can't
8	a are allowed to	b is allowed to	c aren't allowed to

VOCABULARY AND LISTENING

A Phone Call

1 ☆ **You will hear an exchange student in the Netherlands talking about what she likes about the country. Write two questions you'd like to ask.**

____

____

8.01 **2** ☆☆ **Listen to the phone call. Does it answer any of your questions in Exercise 1?**

____

8.01 **3** ☆☆ **Listen again and answer the questions.**

1 What is the subject of the phone call?
studying and living in another country

2 How long will Julia be in the Netherlands?
____

3 What's her favorite thing about life in the Netherlands?
____

4 Why are drivers from the Netherlands usually polite, according to Julia?
____

5 How did Julia travel to school this morning?
____

6 Which country does Julia compare with the Netherlands?
____

Attitude and Behavior

4 ☆ **Complete the words with the correct vowels (*a*, *e*, *i*, *o*, *u*).**

1 r*u*d*e*
2 c_r_f_l
3 _mm_t_r_
4 p_l_t_
5 m_t_r_
6 c_r_l_ss
7 _rg_n_z_d
8 d_s_b_d_ _nt
9 d_s_rg_n_z_d
10 w_ll-b_h_v_d

5 ☆☆ **Complete the sentences with the words in Exercise 4.**

1 Rohan is a very *well-behaved* student: the teachers never need to give him a talk.
2 Patricia is a very ______ child. She never says "please"!
3 Our teacher likes us to be ______ and keep our desks clean and neat.
4 Please be ______ when you cycle in the rain.
5 Don't be ______ – you should check your homework for mistakes before you hand it in.
6 Our parents teach us to be ______ and thank visitors for coming to the house.
7 Bella's pens and pencils are all over the floor. She's so ______ with her things!
8 My little cousin is very ______! My aunt's always giving him a talk, but he never listens.
9 Molly is nearly 16, but sometimes she is very ______ – like a little girl.
10 Paul is younger than his sister Molly, but he's much more ______ and sensible.

6 ☆☆ **Match sentences 1–5 with a–e.**

1 Jorge is so careless. [*c*]
2 He's usually very mature. [ ]
3 Jon's a disobedient boy at home. [ ]
4 Try to be more polite. [ ]
5 Miguel isn't disorganized. [ ]

a He hardly ever does anything that is immature.
b It's so rude not to say "thank you."
c He should try to be more careful.
d His schoolwork is always neat and organized.
e But he's well-behaved at school.

GRAMMAR IN ACTION

To Have To, Must, and To Need To

1 ★ Circle the correct options.

1 You *(need to)* / *don't have to* / *must not* study for exams.

2 He *must* / *doesn't need to* / *doesn't have to* be better-behaved in class – he's very disobedient!

3 Students *don't have to* / *don't need to* / *must not* wear makeup. It's not allowed.

4 We *don't need to* / *have to* / *must not* ask if we don't understand the questions.

5 You *don't have to* / *must* / *have to* finish the essay right now. It's for next week.

2 ★★ Put the words in the correct order to make the Exam FAQs.

Home News FAQs Sign In Register

Exam FAQs

1 need / we / to / an optional question / answer / Do / ?

Do we need to answer an optional question?

2 have / we / Do / to / a pen / use / ?

____

3 do / What / first / need / to / we / do / ?

____

4 if / we / What / have / do / to / do / not sure / we're / ?

____

5 do / need / What / to / we / do / before / finish / we / ?

____

6 have / we / to / Do / the exam room / stay / in / ?

____

4 ★★ Are the sentences about the school notices *T* (true) or *F* (false)? Correct the false sentences with (*don't*) *have to* or *must*(*not*). Sometimes there is more than one possible answer.

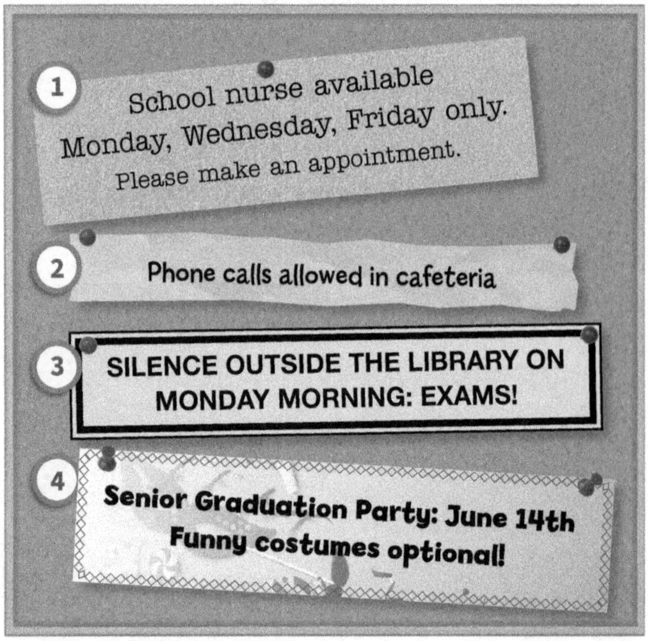

1 You don't have to make an appointment to see the nurse.

F. You have to / must make an appointment to see the nurse.

2 Students don't have to turn off their phones in the cafeteria.

____

3 You must not make noise outside the library on Monday morning.

____

4 Students must wear a funny costume to the graduation party.

____

3 ★★ Complete the sentences with the phrases in the box. Then match the answers (a–f) with the FAQs (1–6) in Exercise 2.

don't have to stay	don't need to answer	have to use	have to write	~~need to check~~	need to read

a You *need to check* all your answers before you finish. ☐

b You ______________ in the room, but please leave quietly. ☐

c You ______________ all the questions carefully before you answer. ☐

d If a question is optional, you ______________ it. ☐

e Yes, you ______________ a black pen. ☐

f You ______________ something, so if you're not sure about an answer, don't leave it blank – guess! ☐

WRITING

An Essay

1 ☆ **Make a list of the advantages and disadvantages of digital technology in school education. Then read the essay. Does it have your ideas?**

____

____

Should We Reduce Digital Technology in the Classroom?

1 Most of us find it difficult to imagine schools without laptops or tablets, but some people believe that using electronic devices in class too much can be a bad thing. [1]<u>essay, / In / outline / I / this</u> some of the advantages and disadvantages of technology and give my own opinion.

2 [2]<u>hand, / the / On / one</u> using digital technology in the classroom can be more exciting than learning from books. Technology can also encourage more students to take part in group work through online activities. It is also believed that using technology can help students remember what they learn.

3 [3]<u>other / On / the / hand,</u> technology may cause students to stop paying attention in class. [4]<u>that / Some / say</u> technology is also bad for social skills, as students might speak to each other less during class. [5]<u>argue / that / Others</u> technology can make cheating easier for students – both in classwork and homework.

4 In my opinion, there are more important advantages than disadvantages, but there should be a balance between technology and traditional classroom work. Computers can never take the place of the teacher!

2 ☆ **Match the parts of the essay (a–d) with the correct paragraphs (1–4).**

a a conclusion with the writer's opinion 4

b bad things about digital technology ___

c an introduction to the topic ___

d good things about digital technology ___

3 ☆☆ **Put the <u>underlined</u> words in the essay in the correct order to make the *Useful Language* phrases.**

1 In this essay, I outline

2 ______________

3 ______________

4 ______________

5 ______________

PLAN

4 ☆☆ **Write your own essay. Look at the title and think of two good things and two bad things about weekend homework. Take notes.**

Is weekend homework a good or bad thing?

Good Things: ______________

____

Bad Things: ______________

____

5 **Decide what to include in each paragraph. Use the information in Exercise 2 to help you.**

WRITE

6 ☆☆☆ **Write your essay. Remember to include four paragraphs, *can/can't*, *to be allowed to*, *to have to*, *must*, *to need to*, and the phrases from the *Useful Language* box (see Student's Book, p101).**

CHECK

7 **Do you …**

- have an introduction and conclusion?
- write about good things and bad things?

8 REVIEW

VOCABULARY

1 Match the beginnings of the sentences (1–6) with the ends (a–f).

1 The teacher will give you a talk if ☐
2 If you study hard for a test, ☐
3 It's always wrong ☐
4 If students don't pay attention, ☐
5 We usually have to write an essay ☐
6 If you study hard, you won't fail ☐

a when we take an English exam.
b the exam – you'll pass it.
c they won't know what to do.
d you'll get a good grade.
e to cheat on a test.
f you don't hand in homework on time.

2 Circle the correct words.

1 Jonty is very *well-behaved / disobedient*: he never gets detention.
2 It's *polite / rude* to talk when your teacher's talking.
3 I'm so *organized / disorganized* that I can never find anything.
4 She's only ten, but she's really *mature / immature* for her age.
5 *Careful / Careless* work doesn't usually get good grades.
6 You're so *well-behaved / disobedient*. You never do anything I tell you!
7 *Immature / Mature* people behave like someone a lot younger.
8 Be *careless / careful* with Ahmet – he's very sensitive!
9 He's very *rude / polite*: he always says "please" and "thank you."
10 Very *organized / disorganized* people plan everything they do.

GRAMMAR IN ACTION

3 Complete the sentences with *can*, *can't*, or the correct form of *to be allowed*.

1 In some countries, girls ________________ go to school because their parents need their help.
2 Boys in that school ________________ to wear long pants. They all wear shorts.
3 We ________________ to have smartphones in the exam room. That's cheating.
4 You ________________ use the library after lunch but not in the morning.
5 If you're late for an exam, you ________________ to take it – you have to do it another day.
6 Your parents ________________ help you because they don't know Latin.

4 Complete the sentences with the words in the box.

have to wear	have to worry	must run	must not run	need to come	need to meet

1 You really ________________. The test starts soon.
2 We don't ________________ school uniforms on the weekend.
3 Sally doesn't ________________. She's studied hard for the test.
4 My parents ________________ my teacher after school.
5 We ________________ in the hallways. It's dangerous.
6 Do I ________________ with you, or can you go alone?

CUMULATIVE GRAMMAR

5 Complete the text with the missing words. Circle the correct options.

HOME ABOUT ME ARCHIVE FOLLOW

Hello! In this week's blog I [1] _____ at exam preparation. Now, if you usually [2] _____ my blog, you'll know that I hate exams. I just [3] _____ do them! If I [4] _____ make exams disappear, I would do it! Anyway, I [5] _____ this subject a lot since my last post, and I think one important thing is planning: you [6] _____ start studying hard before your exams. You [7] _____ start months before, but at least a [8] _____ weeks. You [9] _____ also study at school as well as at home. Find a quiet place, like the library, so you [10] _____ concentrate. Little and often is the best way to study; an hour a day is great. Also, do exercise between study sessions – this helps you relax. I [11] _____ for a run in my local park. Finally, get a good night's sleep before the exam! For my last exam, I [12] _____ well the night before and I got a really bad grade. OK, that's all for now. More tips next week!

	a	b	c
1	look	'm looking	had looked
2	read	will read	have read
3	can	can't to	can't
4	could	can	would
5	'm studying	've studied	'd studied
6	must	don't have to	must to
7	have to	haven't to	don't have to
8	few	little	enough
9	shouldn't	should	should to
10	need to	have to	'll be able to
11	'm going often	go often	often go
12	hadn't slept	haven't slept	wasn't sleeping

9 Where would you go?

VOCABULARY

Travel

1 ★★ **Complete the puzzle. Use the clues.**

1 the place someone is traveling to
2 in or to a different country from yours
3 a family place with hotels, pools, and restaurants
4 when you travel somewhere and go back home in a short time
5 a large boat that you can go on vacation on (two words)
6 when you visit a place and look around it, often with a group of people
7 when you travel from one place to another, usually a long distance
8 a place to stay on vacation, e.g., a hotel, RV, or youth hostel
9 traveling with a large bag, usually visiting many places
10 visiting famous or interesting places on vacation
11 reserve a hotel room or a seat on a plane.

2 ★★ **What are the hidden words in gray in the puzzle in Exercise 1?**

3 ★★ **Complete the text with the correct form of words in Exercise 1. Sometimes more than one answer is possible.**

HOME DESTINATIONS FAQS

If you enjoy going [1] *abroad* and visiting exotic places, then Indonesia is one of the world's most interesting [2] ______. You can fly directly to the capital, Jakarta. Flights can be expensive, so it's best to [3] ______ early. You can also arrive by [4] ______, but this is a much longer [5] ______ by sea through Singapore or Australia. Jakarta is a lively city, and it's just a short [6] ______ by plane to the ancient city of Yogyakarta, where you can go [7] ______ and enjoy old buildings, temples, and even an active volcano. Many tourists go to the island of Bali, which offers many types of [8] ______, from expensive hotels to cheap hostels. You can, of course, stay in a large [9] ______, some with their own restaurants and private beaches. Finally, if you have a lot of time, Indonesia is a popular place to go [10] ______: you could spend months traveling around the country, enjoying the local food and culture.

Explore It!

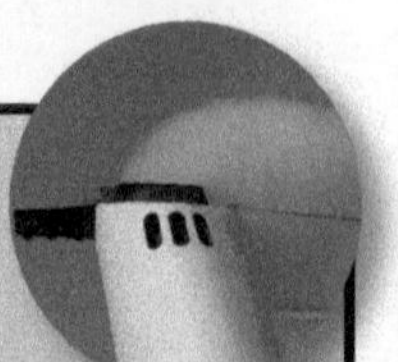

Guess the correct answer.

A cruise ship creates the same amount of pollution in one day as ... cars.

a 5,000 b 20,000 c 1 million

Find another interesting fact about tourism and the environment. Write a question and send it to a classmate in an email, or ask them in the next class.

READING

A Magazine Interview

1 **Look at the photos of drones. Then read the interview and circle the best title.**

a The Dangers of Drones

b Why Drones Will Never Solve Transportation Problems

c How Drones Will Change the Way We Travel

2 **Match the words in bold with the definitions.**

1 staying away from someone or something _avoiding_

2 taking things like food or books to someone's house ________

3 working quickly and in an organized way ________

4 arrive on the ground after moving down through the air ________

5 not having a driver ________

6 big vehicles used to transport things ________

3 **Read the interview again. Complete it with the missing questions.**

Isn't this going to create a lot of problems?

Won't this make people lazy?

What other changes will there be?

~~How will we be traveling in the future?~~

What are the advantages?

4 **Read the interview again. Answer the questions.**

1 How will companies save money with new technology?

They will use driverless trucks.

2 Where might we see flying taxis soon?

____

3 What might be the biggest danger for flying taxis?

____

4 What three things make flying taxis better than normal taxis?

____

____

5 How will drones help people in danger?

____

Computer scientist Jeremy May answers our questions about the future of transportation.

1 _How will we be traveling in the future?_

I think **driverless** taxis will become common. Not only that, but companies will soon be using **trucks** that don't have a driver. This will save companies a lot of money. Some companies have developed a kind of flying taxi, too. It works like a helicopter, but it doesn't need a pilot – it's actually a drone. It's possible that some cities, like Dubai, will have a lot of flying taxis in the near future.

2 ________

Well, some people are worried that driverless taxis aren't safe. Flying taxis have to be even safer, of course. The skies are already full, so one challenge will be **avoiding** objects, like other drones, buildings, and birds. But most of us won't need to worry. It's likely that only the very rich will be able to travel by flying taxi – in the beginning anyway.

3 ________

First, these taxis will use electricity, so they will be more environmentally friendly. Second, they will be able to travel up to 180 kilometers per hour. This, plus the fact that they will be able to take off and **land** anywhere, means that they will be much more **efficient** than normal taxis.

4 ________

Companies will soon start **delivering** things by drone. In Dubai, a company tested a service for people who wanted a coffee but didn't want to travel to a café. The people just ordered online and got their coffee in a few minutes!

5 ________

It might! But the technology has a more serious use. We will be using drones to quickly send medicine or food to difficult-to-reach places like mountains and islands. This will be very useful in emergencies.

GRAMMAR IN ACTION

To Be Going To and Present Continuous for Future

1 ★ Complete the sentences with the phrases in the box. Then write *A* for the arrangements and *P* for the predictions.

| aren't going to find | is going to make |
| ~~'m going to~~ | 're traveling | 's leaving |

1 Next week, I *'m going to* Spain on vacation. *A*
2 He ____________ for the airport in an hour by taxi. ___
3 Technology ____________ travel more environmentally friendly. ___
4 We ____________ to Bali by plane, not cruise ship. ___
5 They ____________ a way to travel that is 100 percent safe. ___

2 ★★ Decide if the sentences are *A* (arrangements) or *P* (predictions). Then complete them with the best form of the verb in parentheses.

1 I *'m meeting* (meet) Ed at four o'clock today. ___
2 She ____________ (not enjoy) the cruise – she hates boats. ___
3 We ____________ (go) camping in July. ___
4 They ____________ (like) Madagascar next summer. The wildlife there is incredible! ___
5 Todd and Laura ____________ (have) lunch at the airport tomorrow before their flight. ___

Future Continuous

3 ★★ Put the words in order to make sentences in the future continuous. Then mark (✓) the sentences you agree with.

1 abroad / in / I / 20 / living / be / years / will
I will be living abroad in 20 years. ☐
2 will / by 2035 / be / traveling / by flying taxi / Everyone
____________ ☐
3 doing / all / Robots / jobs / in / will / be / ten years
____________ ☐
4 50 years / living / other / won't / We / be / planets / on / in
____________ ☐
5 using / won't / be / 15 years / gas / We / in / cars / in
____________ ☐

4 ★★ Circle the best options. For one answer, both options are possible.

I read the other day that we [1]*are living / will be living* on Mars in the next 30 years. Well, you and I [2]*aren't going to live / aren't living* on Mars – they [3]*are only sending / are only going to send* their top astronauts in the near future! Normal people [4]*aren't living / won't be living* there for a long time. The famous scientist Professor Stephen Hawking said that we [5]*are going to need / are needing* to find a new planet in 100 years because we [6]*are having / are going to have* more problems with climate change and other things in the future. I [7]*'m giving / 'm going to give* a presentation on space travel next week at school, so I've done some research! Hawking had previously said that in 1,000 years, people [8]*aren't living / won't be living* on the Earth at all. I'm not sure I agree – a lot of things can happen in 1,000 years!

5 ★★★ Write three predictions in the future continuous. Use the ideas in the box or your own ideas.

communication	houses	music	relationships	work

By 2050, people won't be communicating face-to-face anymore.
____
____
____

VOCABULARY AND LISTENING

Travel Phrasal Verbs

1 ★ **Complete the phrasal verbs in the sentences. Use the words in the box.**

around	away (x2)	back	in	off (x2)	out

1 After we've checked __in__ to our hotel, I want to rest and then have some lunch.

2 We didn't go ________ this summer. We stayed at home for our vacation.

3 I always feel nervous when the plane is taking ________.

4 We have to check ________ of the hotel early – at nine o'clock – but we can leave our bags.

5 Out plane is at 2 p.m., so we need to set ________ for the airport at around 11 a.m.

6 I went to Guadalajara for a short business trip, but I didn't have time to look ________ the city.

7 It's nice to get ________ on vacation once a year and see a new place.

8 Our train was delayed, so we didn't get ________ home until late at night.

9 What time is your plane expected to get ________?

2 ★★ **Complete the email with the correct form of phrasal verbs in Exercise 1.**

Home Inbox Sent **New**

From: Marco To: Carmen

Hello Carmen,

I hope you're well! I'm really looking forward to your visit. What time does your plane [1] __get in__ on Tuesday? Let me know, and I'll [2] ________________ early enough for the airport and pick you up. You won't need to take a taxi. I expect you'll be tired when you arrive, so I'll just let you [3] ________________ to your hotel, and you can relax. You said you wanted to [4] ________________ the city with my parents and me and maybe try some good local restaurants. Unfortunately, my parents are [5] ________________ on business tomorrow. They won't be here when you arrive on Tuesday, but they're going to [6] ________________ the day after. So why don't we all go to a nice restaurant later in the week?

Talk to you soon,

Marco

Conversations

3 ★ **You will hear two people planning a vacation. Look at the map and answer the questions.**

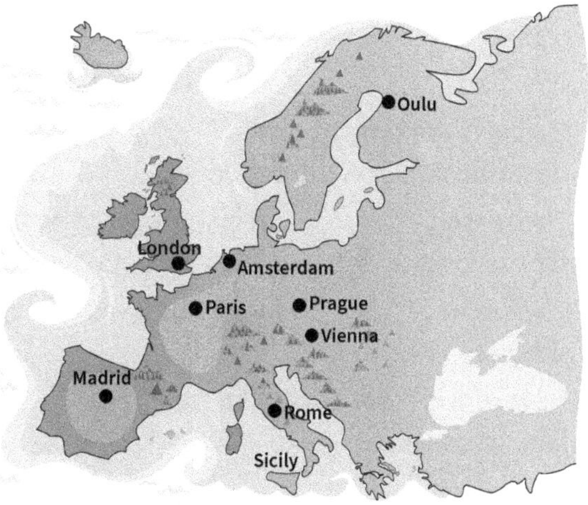

1 Which part of the world are they going to visit?

____

2 What's the best way to travel around and see all these places?

____

3 How much time do you think you would need?

____

9.01 **4** ★ **Listen to the conversation and check your answers to Exercise 3. Do Emma and Mason have the same ideas as you for questions 2 and 3?**

____

9.01 **5** ★★ **Listen again. Are the sentences *T* (true) or *F* (false)?**

1 Emma and Mason can travel anywhere in Europe with their train tickets. __T__

2 Mason wants to go to the beach first. ___

3 Emma would like to visit museums. ___

4 Mason doesn't want to go to Finland because it's cold. ___

5 Mason would like to visit some European capitals. ___

6 Emma doesn't want to go to large cities. ___

GRAMMAR IN ACTION
Relative Pronouns and Relative Clauses

1 ☆ Complete the sentences with relative pronouns.

1 The town _where_ we went on vacation last year was very cheap.
2 The plane __________ I took was two hours late.
3 Spring is the time of year __________ you can see beautiful pink trees in Japan.
4 The reason __________ I want to go to Peru is to try the food.
5 The woman __________ suitcase was damaged was very upset.
6 New York is a good place for people __________ like sightseeing.

2 ☆☆ Correct one mistake in each sentence.

1 I remember the time where we went to London to see the Houses of Parliament.
I remember the time when we went to London to see the Houses of Parliament.
2 This is the resort I will be staying.
____
3 Is that the girl who bag got lost?
____
4 I lost the camera I brought it with me.
____
5 I have an app on my phone what tells me about all the best tourist attractions.
____
6 Mark is the person who I'm going to visit him in London.
____

3 ☆☆ Complete the text with the clauses in the box and the correct relative pronouns.

brings you	has traveled to lots of countries	I can see
I got a package in the mail	~~I want to visit Japan~~	opinion I trust

The reason [1] _why I want to visit Japan_ is my brother Jonathan. He's someone [2] __________, including the U.S.A. and Australia, but he always says that Japan is his favorite place. He was working there when I was really young, and he often used to send me presents. I loved the moment [3] __________, and there was something inside, like a cool toy, food, or a *maneki-neko* (this is like a little cat [4] __________ good luck). So, Jonathan is the person [5] __________ the most about traveling to different countries – I always ask him for advice. I hope I can visit Tokyo one day and also other smaller towns [6] __________ traditional Japanese life.

4 ☆☆☆ Join the sentences using a relative pronoun.

1 These are the people. I met them on vacation.
These are the people who I met on vacation.
2 France is the country. It has more tourists than any other country.
____
3 The departures lounge is a place in an airport. You wait for your plane there.
____
4 Drones are a new invention. They might replace normal taxis.
____
5 Norway is the place. I will be traveling there next summer.
____
6 Check-out is the time. We need to leave the hotel.
____
7 Linda is the person. Her brother is a pilot.
____

WRITING

An Email to a Host Family

1 ★ **Read the email quickly. Mark (✓) the information that Bedour wants to find out.**

1 where Boston is ☐
2 what she will study in the course ☐
3 where she can find a place to stay ☐
4 when the course starts ☐
5 when the course finishes ☐
6 how to travel to Boston ☐

2 ★ **Put a–e in the order they appear in Bedour's email (1–5).**

a ☐ goodbye
b ☐ questions about the trip
c [1] greeting
d ☐ reason for writing
e ☐ thanks

3 ★★ **Complete the email with the *Useful Language* phrases.**

a Best wishes
b ~~Dear~~
c Do you know
d I'm writing to
e thank you very much for

PLAN

4 ★★ **Write your own email to a school abroad. First, decide what you are going to study and where. Write questions to ask your course organizer about these things.**

Your Travel Plans and When You Arrive:

____

____

Your Accommodation:

____

____

Your Course Content and Timetable:

____

____

5 **Decide what information to include. Use the information in Exercise 2 to help you.**

WRITE

6 ★★★ **Write your email. Remember to include *to be going to*, the present continuous, the future continuous, and phrases from the *Useful Language* box (see Student's Book, p113).**

CHECK

7 **Do you …**

- use a greeting at the beginning and say goodbye at the end?
- say why you are writing?
- say thank you?

Home Inbox Sent **New**

From: bedour2004@mymail.com

Subject: Summer Course

1 Dear Mr. Hamilton,

I hope you're well. 2 ________________ check some details about my visit to Boston this summer. I'm looking forward to starting the course, and I hope I'm going to really improve my English!

As you may know, this is going to be my first time in the U.S.A. Is it possible to ask some questions? I received your welcome pack that gives information about accommodations. Unfortunately, the places that were listed all look a long way from the center of Boston. 3 ________________ if I could find somewhere closer? I'd prefer not to spend too much time traveling each day.

I'd also like to ask about the exact dates of the course. I know the course will be starting on June 25, but do I have to arrive earlier? Could you also tell me when the course ends, exactly? I'm asking because it's important for me to book my flights.

Finally, 4 ________________ accepting me into this course. My family is so happy for me!

5 ________________,

Bedour

9 REVIEW

VOCABULARY

1 Match the beginnings of the sentences (1–8) with the ends (a–h).

1 We arrived at our final ☐
2 I didn't stay in my own country for my last vacation; I went ☐
3 People like to visit the old market in my city – it's a popular ☐
4 I stayed in a big ☐
5 We went on several day ☐
6 I went online and ☐
7 If I had a lot of time, I'd like to ☐
8 Hotels, hostels, or villas: any ☐

a trips to local towns.
b abroad.
c accommodation is OK for me.
d resort, and my room looked out over the beach.
e destination on time.
f go backpacking across the country.
g tourist attraction.
h booked tickets for my trip next week.

2 Underline and correct six travel phrasal verbs in the sentences. Mark (✓) the correct sentences.

1 You need to check on at the airport two hours before your flight. ________________
2 Please check in of the hotel right after breakfast, no later. ________________
3 My plane gets in at five o'clock in the morning. I'm going to be so tired! ________________
4 We're going out on vacation next week. Can you take care of our cat? ________________
5 My dad is on a business trip right now, but he'll get away tonight. ________________
6 I looked on the city, but everything was closed. ________________
7 After the plane took out, I had an amazing view from the window. ________________
8 What time are you setting off for the airport tomorrow morning? ________________

GRAMMAR IN ACTION

3 Complete the sentences with the correct form of the verbs in the box. Use the tense in parentheses.

have	live	meet	not learn	study	visit

1 Next week, I ________________ lunch with my grandparents. (present continuous)
2 This time next year, I hope I ________________ science at college. (future continuous)
3 Some people think that we ________________ on other planets in the future. (future continuous)
4 We ________________ a lot of interesting places on vacation, I'm sure. (*to be going to*)
5 My host family ________________ me at the airport at six o'clock. (present continuous)
6 Emma ________________ much Spanish; she's only staying in Madrid for two weeks. (*to be going to*)

4 **Write sentences using the correct relative pronoun from the options in parentheses.**

1 The person was sitting near me on the plane is a famous actor! (who / whose)

____

2 I stayed at a resort is one of the best in the country. (why / that)

____

3 That's the passenger father is the pilot. (who / whose)

____

4 Cambodia is a country you can visit a lot of interesting old cities. (where / that)

____

5 The main reason I want to visit Italy is all the great food. (which / why)

____

6 June and July is a time there is a lot of rain in Japan. (when / where)

____

CUMULATIVE GRAMMAR

5 **Complete the text with the missing words. Circle the correct options.**

Usually, it only takes about 12 hours to fly from the UK to Thailand. That's not [1]______, but so far it's been 32 hours [2]______ I left home! I had set off for the airport early. I wanted to relax after checking in. After I [3]______ in, the first thing I saw on the screens was that my flight [4]______! At first, it was only two hours, then four, then eight! I [5]______ that there were problems with the airplane. It [6]______ in London yet. It was still in Moscow – about five hours away! The airline told me I [7]______ stay in a hotel near the airport and they would pay for it. At 3 a.m., I [8]______ a phone call saying that my plane had arrived, and that [9]______ I went immediately to the airport, I would miss the flight! I got on the plane, and many hours later it landed at a new destination – Dhaka, the capital of Bangladesh! My plane needed [10]______ some other passengers. I'm still in Dhaka now! [11]______ here for four hours so far! I [12]______ think that traveling was fun, but now I'm not so sure!

	a	b	c
1	long enough	enough long	too long
2	since	for	from
3	have checked	check	had checked
4	was delayed	delayed	is delayed
5	was told	was said	told
6	hasn't arrived	didn't arrive	hadn't arrived
7	can	could	would
8	get	got	was getting
9	if	when	unless
10	to pick up	picking up	pick up
11	I was	I've been	I'd been
12	used to	use to	did use to

EXAM TIPS: Reading Skills

Reading: Multiple Matching

You will read short descriptions of five people and match them with the best options. The options typically give information about places, services, entertainment, restaurants, etc.

There are eight options for five people, so there will be three extra. These extra options usually fit only partially.

Exam Guide: Multiple Matching

- To do this task, you should first read through the short description of each person. You should then decide what the most important information about each one is and underline it.
- Before reading through the options, think about what sort of thing you would recommend for each person. For example, if they like eating fish, you might recommend a restaurant that specializes in fish dishes.
- Then read through each option and underline the important information.
- Always double-check and read the information carefully. Are there any traps? For example, a young man might be looking for a summer job on an organic farm and one of the options offers this. But beware! The young man also says he wants to improve his **French** and the job is in **Spain**, so it is not the perfect match.
- Be careful not to "word spot." If the same word is in the description and in one of the options, it might be a trap and not a match.

REMEMBER!

Make sure the text you choose matches all the requirements in the person's description.

Reading Practice: Multiple Matching

Tip! The descriptions and the texts often have the same information, but they are written using different words.

1 Read the text and match the words in bold with the words in the box.

accommodation	easygoing	famous	secretary
said we were sorry	said we would	star	talk show

I can really recommend the vacation [1]**apartment** in Pocos, where we spent two weeks. The owner is a TV [2]**celebrity** who has a popular late-night [3]**chat show** and is very [4]**well-known** in Brazil. We didn't meet her, but her [5]**assistant** was waiting for us when we arrived. We [6]**apologized** for being so late, but he was very friendly and [7]**not at all difficult**. We [8]**promised to** write a good review when we left!

1 ______ 4 ______ 7 ______

2 ______ 5 ______ 8 ______

3 ______ 6 ______

2 Look at the word in bold in each sentence and choose the option you think has the closest meaning.

1 That actor played the **lead** in a movie we went to see last week.

A director B hero C role

2 Parents shouldn't be too **harsh** with teenagers at exam time.

A strict B proud C miserable

3 This restaurant offers a wide **range** of vegetarian and vegan options.

A variety B line C sort

4 He works with a team of exciting and **innovative** young designers.

A athletic B creative C gentle

Tip!

Sometimes you have to guess the meaning of a word you don't know. Look at the context by reading the words and sentences that come before and after the word.

Tip!

Look out for traps! A useful way to check if your answer is correct is to think about why the other options are incorrect.

3 Read the descriptions of two people. Answer the questions.

A Gabriela wants to study English at a language school in Cambridge, where she has an aunt she can stay with. She loves soccer and wants to play on a team. Her language level is not very advanced, but she is very excited to learn. She wants small classes of mixed nationalities so that she has to speak English with her classmates.

B Winston is 25. He is very good at soccer and has played professionally. Now he wants to be a gym teacher, so he needs a teaching certificate in different sports. He is looking for a college outside a city with good sporting facilities and cheap college accommodation.

1 Which description mentions accommodation: A, B, or both?

2 Which description mentions student accommodation: A, B, or both?

3 Which person likes sports, especially soccer? Gabriela, Winston, or both?

4 Which person wants to teach sports? Gabriela, Winston, or both?

4 Read the descriptions of two colleges. Answer the questions.

Greystones College was built in 2003 in an attractive open area in the country just outside of Oxford. Places are available for our language-learning courses, which are taught in small numbers or intensively, one-on-one. Students stay with local families to give them the greatest opportunities to practice their language skills. There are good sporting and social activities all year round.

Hinton College is located in Cambridge, one of the UK's oldest and most beautiful university cities. The college has a a high level of success in English language learning. Our beginner classes are taught in groups of three or four by qualified native speakers. Social activities are arranged as part of the course, and team sports are encouraged. All of our courses are from one to six months in length.

1 Underline four important facts about each college:

- where they are
- what courses they offer
- how big the classes are
- what other activities they offer

2 What information tells you Greystones College is not suitable for Gabriela?

3 What information tells you Hinton College is suitable for Gabriela?

EXAM TIPS: Writing Skills

Writing: An Email

Writing an Email Response

For this question, you are given a short message from an English-speaking friend. You have to respond to the message in around 100 words. This tests your ability to understand a message and to write a clear response.

Exam Guide: Writing an Email

- Read the instructions carefully so that you understand who you are writing to and why you are writing.
- Your answer should be around 100 words. Don't write much more or much less than that.
- Begin and end your email correctly. Use:
  - your friend's name
  - an opening phrase.
  - one sentence for each point from the original email
  - a phrase to close
  - your name at the end.
- Start your sentences in different ways to make your email interesting.
- Don't copy too much language from the question. Try to think of synonyms where possible.

Writing Practice: Writing an Email

1 Read the instructions and the statements that follow. Are the statements true or false?

You are planning to visit your friend Robin in Canada. Read Robin's message. Then write an email to him.

From: Robin
Subject: Your trip!
Hi there!
I'm so happy to hear you are coming to visit me. You are going to love Canada!
On the first weekend you are here would you like to go ice-skating or to see a hockey game?
Let me know what kind of food you like to eat so we can buy it from the store. And don't forget to bring warm clothes. In January it's going to be freezing.
Can't wait to see you.
Bye!
Robin

	True	False
1 Your friend Robin is in Canada.	☐	☐
2 The message is from Robin.	☐	☐
3 Robin is planning to visit you.	☐	☐
4 You might go see a hockey game.	☐	☐
5 Robin has bought some food for you.	☐	☐
6 Your answer should be in email form.	☐	☐

2 **Read the sentences from two emails from the same boy. One is to his teacher, and the other to his friend. In your notebooks, write them in the correct order under the right heading, formal or informal.**

Formal	Informal

> **Tip!** Make sure you use the appropriate style: it should not be formal if you're writing to a friend.

I hope to be back at school on Monday.
I have a very bad cold and a high temperature.
Dear Mr. Jacobs,
Yours truly, Michael Fanshaw
Can you please send me this week's homework?
I apologize for my absence from class yesterday.

Bye, Mike
See you next week with any luck.
I have an awful cold – I'm coughing and sweating.
Hi Ana,
Let me know if there's any homework, OK?
Sorry I wasn't there yesterday.

3 **Change the words in bold to make the sentences more interesting. Use the words in the box or your own ideas.**

> **Tip!** Use a range of vocabulary: make sure you don't use the same word too many times.

amazing awesome boring colorful cool freezing great hate love pleasant prefer rainy

1 There's a **good** skate park with a **good** café near my home.

____

2 We had a **nice** camping vacation, but the weather was **not nice**.

____

3 I **like** swimming, but if you **don't like** it we can do something you'd **like more**.

____

4 The art galleries in my town are **not very interesting**, but the Museum of Tomorrow is **very interesting.**

____

5 We could go to the parade. It's very **nice** and the costumes are usually **nice**.

____

4 **Correct the mistake in each sentence.**

> **Tip!** Check your writing for any mistakes in spelling or grammar.

1 Don't forget turn off the lights when you leave.

____

2 Are you scared thunder and lightning?

____

3 The weather forecast says it's going snowing tonight.

____

4 I can't sing because I have a very hurt throat.

____

EXAM TIPS: Listening Skills

Listening: Multiple Choice

You will listen to short unrelated extracts and choose from three options. This tests your ability to listen for specific information and answer a question about what you hear.

Exam Guide: Three-Option Multiple Choice

- Use the time before you listen to read the questions. Read them carefully because they tell you what you need to listen for.
- All the possible answers may be in the recording, but only one will answer the question.
- Focus on the general meaning of what you hear. You may have to listen for the person's opinion, which is not necessarily a single word or phrase.
- If you're not sure, mark the answers you think are possible and check on the second listening.
- Always give an answer, even if you're still not sure. A guess might be right.
- Use the second listening to check, even if you're sure you're right. Don't stop listening!

REMEMBER!

You will hear the instructions on the recording. Listen carefully and read the question at the same time because this will help you understand the topic and the context.

Listening Practice: Multiple Choice

1 Underline two key words or phrases in each question.

1 What time does the girl's exam start?
2 What is the man going to buy?
3 Which evening activity is for beginners?
4 Why did Caroline leave her job?
5 Where are the teacher's keys?
6 What did Hari do this morning?

Tip! Underline the key words in the question. Then listen for the words that mean the same as the key words.

E.01 **2 You will hear a teenage girl speaking to her mother about an exam. Read the question below.**

What time does the girl's exam start?

A It starts at 11:30.

B Four o'clock.

C It begins at nine.

Tip! If the recording is a conversation, listen for the right person: who does the question refer to?

Now listen to the conversation. Why are options A and B not correct?

____

____

3 **You will hear two people talking about a play they've just seen. What words do you expect to hear in connection with the three options? Choose from the words in the box or use your own ideas.**

bad boring great impressive interesting
old-fashioned too long too short

The Length	The Acting	The Costumes

E.02 **4** **Listen to the conversation and answer the questions.**

1 What did the woman think about the play?

A She thought the play was too long.

B She thought it was very disappointing.

C She liked the actors.

2 What did the man think of the costumes?

A He thought they were old-fashioned.

B He likes fifties fashion.

C He thought the clothes were terrible.

3 When is the play supposed to be set?

A the 1950s

B It's not mentioned.

C in the present

Adverbs of Frequency

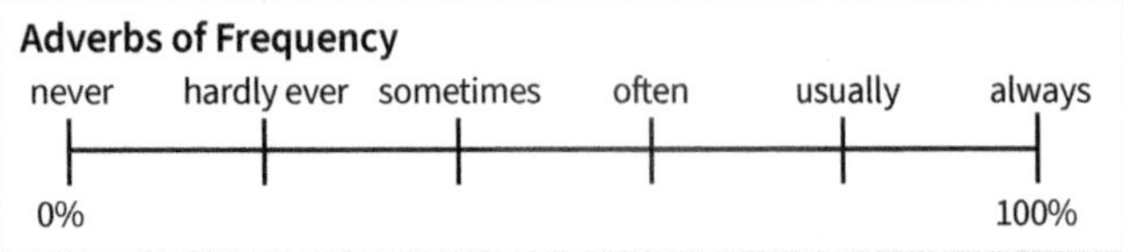

- We use **adverbs of frequency** to say how often something happens.
- We put them before the main verb but after the verb ***to be***.
  I often text my friends.
  There are always music festivals in the summer.
- ***Often, sometimes,*** and ***usually*** can also come at the beginning of the sentence.
  Sometimes, my family, and I listen to music.

Expressions of Frequency

every	day / week / weekend / year
once / twice / three times	a day / a week / a month / a year

- We also use **expressions of frequency** to say how often something happens.
- We usually place them after the verb phrase, but they can also come at the beginning or end of a sentence.
  I see my friends twice a week.
  Every weekend, they give a concert.
- We can use an expression of frequency and an adverb of frequency in the same sentence.
  I usually go on vacation once a year.

Simple Present and Present Continuous

- We use the **simple present** to talk about facts, habits, and routines.
  My sister likes rock music.
  I use my phone every day.
- We use **adverbs of frequency** (***always***, ***often***, etc.) with the **simple present** and ***at the moment*** and ***now*** with the **present continuous**.
  My dad often plays computer games with me.
  My teacher is walking into the classroom now.
- We also use the **simple present** to talk about future planned events if a **future time expression** is used or understood.
  My mom starts work at 10 a.m. on Friday.
  Hannah can't come shopping with me this afternoon.
- We can also use the **present continuous** to talk about temporary future plans or arrangements.
  We are taking a trip to Florida.

Simple Past: Regular and Irregular Verbs

	Affirmative	Negative
I / He / She / It We / You / They	called me.	didn't call me.

Questions		
Did	I / he / she / it / we / you / they	call you?

Short Answers		
Yes,	I / he / she / it / we / you / they	did.
No,	I / he / she / it / we / you / they	didn't.

- We use the **simple past** to talk about completed events and actions in the past.
  I watched the band play last night.
  Three years ago, she had a great party.
- To form the affirmative of the **simple past**, we add *-ed* or *-d* to the infinitive.
  help – helped *organize – organized* *play – played*
- For verbs ending **consonant** + ***-y***, remove the *-y* and add *-ied*.
  study – studied *cry – cried* *try – tried*
- For one-syllable verbs ending **consonant** + **vowel** + **consonant**, we double the final consonant and add *-ed*.
  drop – dropped *chat – chatted*
  For verbs that have two or more syllables, double the final consonant and add *-ed* if the stress is on the last syllable. If the stress is not on the last syllable, do not double the consonant before adding *-ed*.
  tra*vel* – *traveled* *pre****fer*** – *preferred*
  We do not double the consonant in words that end in *w*, *x*, *y*, or *z*.
  tow - towed *relax - relaxed*
- Many common verbs are irregular in the **simple past**.
  get – got *put – put*
  have – had *make – made*
- Question words always go at the beginning of the question.
  When did the concert start?
  Where was your brother last night?

Simple Present and Present Continuous with Adverbs of Frequency

1 Put the words in parentheses in the correct place in the sentence.

1 Do you play in a band on Saturday nights? (always)

Do you always play in a band on Saturday nights?

2 We see our friends at the jazz club in town. (sometimes)

___

3 My mom gets angry with me when I'm late. (never)

___

4 I text my teacher when I can't do my homework. (hardly ever)

___

5 My brother's soccer team wins the cup. (often)

___

6 Are those music apps free or not? (usually)

___

2 Complete the sentences with the correct form of the verbs in the box.

do	go	have	~~post~~	spend	study

1 *Does* your sister usually *post* photos on social media?

2 I'm on vacation at the moment and I ______ a great time!

3 How much money ______ you usually ______ each week?

4 What ______ your parents ______ when you get good grades at school?

5 We ______ by bus today because it's too cold to walk.

6 She ______ for exams this weekend, so she doesn't have much free time.

Simple Present and Present Continuous for Future

3 Put the words in the correct order to make sentences about the future.

1 eight / English / at / starts / class / Our / thirty

Our English class starts at eight thirty.

2 begin / time / the / does / tomorrow / What / concert / ?

___

3 taking / next week / My / Chicago / grandparents / train / to / the / are

___

4 six / This / closes / tonight / at / store

___

5 the / trip / We / for / morning / leaving / our / in / are

___

6 back / teacher / week / We / our / next / essays / the / get / from

___

Simple Past

4 Use the prompts to make questions and answers in the simple past.

1 When / you see that movie? / last week

When did you see that movie? I/We saw it last week.

2 What time / the girls go to bed? / after 11

___

3 Where / your parents meet? / in college

___

4 What / he buy yesterday? / a new bike

___

5 How / the visitors get here? / by boat

___

6 When / the last bus leave? / at ten

___

Simple Past and Past Continuous with *When* and *While*

	Affirmative	Negative	
I / He / She / It	was crying.	wasn't crying.	
We / You / They	were crying.	weren't crying.	
Questions			
Was	I / he / she / it	crying?	
Were	we / you / they		
Short Answers			
Yes,	I / he / she / it		was.
	we / you / they		were.
No,	I / he / she / it		wasn't.
	we / you / they		weren't.

- We use the **past continuous** to talk about actions in progress around a time in the past.
  At seven o'clock, I was waiting for the bus.
  Chloe was wearing jeans yesterday.
- We also use ***when*** and ***while*** to mean "during that time" or to connect two events happening at the same time.
  When my parents were studying, they didn't have the Internet.
  While he was eating, the phone rang.
- We usually use ***while*** with the past continuous to emphasize an ongoing action in the past.
- We usually use ***when*** with the simple past to talk about an interrupting action.

Used To

	Affirmative	Negative
I / He / She / It / We / You / They	used to play soccer.	didn't use to play soccer.
Questions and Short Answers		
Did	I / he / she / it / we / you / they	use to be scared?
Yes,	I / he / she / it / we / you / they	did.
No,		didn't.

- ***Used to*** emphasizes that past states, habits, and actions are now finished.
  It used to be a library, but now it's a museum.
  We used to walk to school, but now we ride our bikes.
- We do not use ***used to*** to talk about things that only happened once, how many times something happened, or duration.
  They went to the movies yesterday.
  ~~*They used to go to the movies yesterday.*~~
  My brother lived there for four years.
  ~~*My brother used to live there for four years.*~~
- ***Used to*** does not have a present form. For present habits and states, we use the simple present.
  My cousin drinks coffee in the morning.

Simple Past and Past Continuous with *When* and *While*

1 Complete the sentences with the past continuous form of the verbs in the box.

cook	look	not study	~~snow~~	wear

1 It ___was snowing___ all day yesterday, so we didn't play soccer.
2 We ______ for you after class. Where were you?
3 Marcos ______ – he was reading a magazine!
4 Nina ______ her new shoes for the first time.
5 What ______ you ______ in the kitchen earlier? It didn't smell very good!

2 Write sentences with *when* or *while* and the correct form of the verbs. Some sentences can have more than one answer.

1 Her father / wait / she arrive home
Her father was waiting when she arrived home.
2 The doorbell / ring / I make tea
______
3 The boys / walk home / their teacher drive past
______
4 Our friends / arrive / we prepare lunch
______
5 I / listen to music / I do my homework
______

3 Circle the correct option.

1 What *did they do* / *were they doing* when *we called* / *were calling* them?
2 She *watched* / *was watching* a movie when her computer *broke* / *was breaking*.
3 I *didn't see* / *wasn't seeing* you while I *shopped* / *was shopping* in town.
4 The police *stopped* / *were stopping* her when she *drove* / *was driving* to work.
5 We *walked* / *were walking* to school when the rain *started* / *was starting*.
6 They *shouted* / *were shouting* for ages, but nobody *heard* / *was hearing* them.

4 Complete the conversation with the correct past form of the verbs in parentheses.

JORGE Hi, Lena! [1] ___Did you finish___ (you / finish) your history essay yesterday?
LENA No, I [2] ______ (work) on it after school when my mom [3] ______ (stop) me.
JORGE Why [4] ______ (she / do) that?
LENA Because she [5] ______ (want) me to help her with dinner. Then I [6] ______ (watch) a wildlife show on TV.
JORGE Oh, yeah. I [7] ______ (see) that! So then I guess you [8] ______ (be) too tired!
LENA Correct!

Used To

5 Make sentences with the correct form of *used to* and the verbs in the box.

~~have~~	live	not eat	play

1 1 Our neighbors ___used to have___ a horse.
2 We ______ in a smaller apartment.
3 Children ______ outside until it got dark.
4 Ollie ______ vegetables, but he does now.

6 Make questions to match the answers.

1 Did you use to go to school by bus?
No, not by bus. I went to school by bike.
2 ______?
No, my sister's never eaten meat.
3 ______?
No, my sister played with me, but not my brother.
4 ______?
Olives? No, and I still hate them!

7 Circle the correct options.

School teachers in the 1950s [1] *used to write* / *used writing* on chalkboards because, of course, they [2] *didn't have* / *weren't having* today's technology. They [3] *used to talk* / *did talk* a lot while the children [4] *were sitting* / *didn't sit* quietly. School books never [5] *didn't use to look* / *looked* very interesting, and there weren't any videos to watch. Many teachers [6] *used to be* / *were being* stricter than they are now, too.

GRAMMAR REFERENCE UNIT 2

Present Perfect: Regular Verbs

Affirmative / Negative			Questions		
I / We / You / They	have walked / haven't walked	to school.	Have	I / we / you / they	walked to school?
He / She / It	has walked / hasn't walked		Has	he / she / it	
Short Answers					
Yes,	I / we / you / they	have.	No,	I / we / you / they	haven't.
	he / she / it	has.		he / she / it	hasn't.

- We use the **present perfect** to talk about actions, experiences, and facts in the past, when the exact time is not mentioned or important.
  The orchestra has played in many countries.
  He has visited the art exhibition.
- We form the affirmative with **subject** + ***have*/*has*** + **past participle**.
  I've talked to Danielle. *She's asked me for help.*
- We form the negative with **subject** + ***haven't*/*hasn't*** + **past participle**.
  Max hasn't auditioned for the part.
  They haven't performed in front of an audience.
- We form questions in the **present perfect** with ***have*/*has*** + **subject** + **past participle**. We often use ***ever*** in present perfect questions to ask about your whole life.
  Has she ever had drum lessons?
  Have you ever been to the theater?
- We often use ***never*** to say "not at any time" when answering these questions.
  A: *Has he ever met a famous person?* **B:** *No, never.*
- Regular past participles end in *-ed*, *-d*, or *-ied*.
  want – wanted *believe – believed* *worry – worried*

Present Perfect: Irregular Verbs

- Many common verbs have irregular past participles.
  go – gone *put – put* *be – been* *make – made*
  see – seen *hear – heard*
- We use ***go*** (***gone***) for physical actions, to say somebody has not returned from a place or from doing an activity. We use ***be*** (***been***) for completed experiences, to say somebody has returned from a place or from doing an activity.
  They've gone to Rome. (*They are in Rome now.*)
  They've been to Rome. (*They have returned.*)

Present Perfect with *Already*, *Just*, *Still*, and *Yet*

- We often use ***already***, ***just***, ***still***, and ***yet*** with the present perfect.
  Jack has already been to the exhibition twice.
  Emily has just started learning Spanish.
  We still haven't chosen a movie to watch.
  I haven't had time to go shopping yet.
- We use ***already*** to explain that something happened before we expected or to emphasize it has happened. We normally put ***already*** between ***have/has*** and the **past participle**.
  She has already bought a ticket.
  I have already seen the show.
- We use ***just*** with the present perfect to talk about very recent events and actions.
  I've just heard the good news. It's fantastic!
  Dad's just gotten home and he's feeling tired.
- We use ***still*** in negative sentences to express that something we expected has not happened, but we imagine it will happen in the future. We put ***still*** directly after the subject.
  My uncle still hasn't seen the new play.
- We use ***yet*** in negative sentences to emphasize that something we expected has not happened. We put ***yet*** after the complete verb phrase.
  John hasn't arrived yet.
  I haven't asked my parents for permission yet.
- We use ***yet*** in questions to ask if something has happened before now. It comes at the end of the question.
  Have you bought the bus tickets yet?
- In short answers in the negative, we say ***Not yet***.
  A: *Have you spoken to the drama teacher?* **B:** *Not yet.*

Present Perfect with Regular and Irregular Verbs

1 Complete the sentences with the present perfect form of the verbs in parentheses.

1 A TV celebrity has opened (open) a new supermarket in our town.
2 This Chinese circus ______ (not perform) in South America before.
3 I ______ (look) everywhere, but I can't find my phone.
4 ______ the DJ ______ (play) your favorite song?
5 Our teacher ______ (work) as a filmmaker.
6 ______ they ______ (invite) you to their exhibition?

2 Complete the sentences with *been* or *gone*.

1 We've been on vacation. We came home yesterday.
2 Felix has ______ to Brazil three times.
3 The children have ______ out, but they won't be late.
4 I've ______ shopping. Please help me with my bags.
5 Where's Jared? Has he ______ to bed?
6 My mom's not here. She's ______ to work.

3 Write questions with the present perfect and the phrases in the box. Then write true answers.

~~be to a science museum~~	make a sculpture	
see a ballet	take music lessons	win a prize

1 Have you ever been to a science museum?
Yes, I have. / No, I haven't.
2 ______
3 ______
4 ______
5 ______

Present Perfect with *Already*, *Just*, *Still*, and *Yet*

4 Put the words in the correct order to make sentences.

1 written / I've / some / lyrics / just / cool
I've just written some cool lyrics.
2 *Hamlet* / seen / a / just / of / She's / performance
3 song / We / just / our / first / recorded / have
4 the / started / just / They've / rehearsal
5 auditioned / a / for / show / a / just / Mina / has / part / in

5 Circle the correct sentences.

1 (a) She still hasn't played in a professional orchestra.
b She yet hasn't played in a professional orchestra.
2 a The concert tickets haven't arrived yet.
b The concert tickets haven't arrived still.
3 a Have you read this review? No, already not.
b Have you read this review? No, not yet.
4 a Janek has already seen that movie twice.
b Janek has still seen that movie twice.

6 Put the words in parentheses in the correct position in the sentences.

1 Esma has heard from the movie director. (just)
Esma has just heard from the movie director.
2 Has she had her audition? (yet)
3 Yes, she's had an audition and an interview (already).
4 Has she heard what part she's gotten? (yet)
5 No, the director hasn't told her. (still)

Can, Could, Will Be Able To

- We often use ***can*** to talk about ability to do something in the present.
  She can speak English and Polish.
- We often use ***could*** to talk about ability to do something in the past.
  People could visit the museum for free last week.
- We often use ***will be able to*** to talk about ability to do something in the future.
  I will be able to translate this document tomorrow.

Present Perfect with *How long ... ?* and *For/Since*

How long ... ?

- We use ***How long ... ?*** with the **present perfect** to ask about the duration of a state or activity.
  A: *How long have you known Greg?*
  B: *I've known him since 2012.*

For* and *Since

- We use ***for*** and ***since*** with the **present perfect** to say how long something has been true.
  She hasn't lived in Santiago for three years.
  I've lived here since I was seven.
- We use ***for*** with periods of time.
  Liam's had a new bike for three days.
  My parents have been married for 21 years.
- We use ***since*** with a reference to a specific time.
  We've been best friends since 2009.
  Emma and Anna haven't seen each other since June.

Present Perfect and Simple Past

- We use the **simple past** when the moment in which something happened has ended. When it happened isn't always mentioned, usually because it is clear.
  I went to Monterrey in June. (It's now July.)
  They began the exam two minutes ago. (It's now 10:02, not 10:00.)
  She wanted to ask you a question. (when I spoke to her)
- We use the **present perfect** when something started or happened in the past and continues to be true until now. We can say how long something has been true but not when it started.
  I've been to Monterrey. (*When isn't specified, but it continues to be true.*)
  They've begun the exam. (*and the exam hasn't finished*)
  She's wanted to ask you a question for a few days.
  (*She continues to want to.*)

GRAMMAR PRACTICE UNIT 3

Can, Could, Will Be Able To

1 Are the sentences about the *P* (past), *Pr* (present), or *F* (future)?

1 We won't be able to wave goodbye when they leave. F
2 I can translate the instructions for you. ___
3 He will be able to come to the meeting. ___
4 My parents couldn't understand their Brazilian guests. ___
5 She couldn't hear her phone, so she didn't answer. ___
6 We can't wait or we'll miss our bus. ___

2 Complete the text with the correct form of *can*, *could*, or *will be able to*.

> Beatriz comes from São Paulo, so she [1] can speak Brazilian Portuguese very well. She speaks English fairly well, but she [2] ________ always understand if people talk too fast. When she was younger, she [3] ________ speak Spanish, but she studied it in school and now she [4] ________. Next year, she's going to stay with an aunt in Luzern. She [5] ________ learn Swiss German there, but she [6] ________ understand people in the French- and Italian-speaking regions of the country.

3 Circle the correct options.

1 We … hear the speaker because he's talking quietly.
a could b couldn't (c) can't
2 Antonio is so good at languages. He … speak a lot of them!
a will be able to b could c can
3 My parents … choose to learn Greek or Latin when they were at school.
a could b can c can't
4 I hope I … help you later. I'll be free this evening.
a can't b will be able to c could
5 We … see the video if we miss the next class.
a couldn't b won't be able to c can to
6 … visit the Art Institute when you're in Chicago next week?
a Able you to b Can you able to c Will you be able to

Present Perfect with *How long … ?* and *For/Since*

4 Complete the sentences with *for* or *since*.

1 I have known my friend Victoria for four years.
2 She hasn't seen her grandparents ________ a long time.
3 We've lived in this apartment ________ 2016.
4 Have you been at home ________ lunchtime?

5 Make questions with *How long* and the correct form of the verb.

1 you / be at this school?
How long have you been at this school?
2 she / know her best friend?
____
3 they / live near you?
____
4 Lucas / have that phone?
____

Present Perfect and Simple Past

6 Circle the correct options.

1 My mother (*has worked*) / *worked* at this museum since 2004.
2 He *has told* / *told* me the same joke yesterday.
3 They *haven't begun* / *didn't begin* the exam yet.
4 *Has she ever told* / *Did she ever tell* lies before?

7 Complete the conversation with the correct form of the verbs in parentheses.

LUIS Sorry I'm late, Alan. How long [1] have you been (be) here?
ALAN No problem, I [2] ________ (just get) here.
LUIS [3] ________ the teacher ________ (arrive) yet?
ALAN No, not yet. She [4] ________ (tell) us yesterday that she might be late.
LUIS Oh, did she? I [5] ________ (not hear) that. Your English is very good!
ALAN Thanks! I [6] ________ (study) it since fifth grade.

Quantifiers

Countable	Uncountable
a few	a little
enough	enough
too many	too much

- We use **quantifiers** to talk about the amount of something.
- We use ***a few*** and ***a little*** to express small quantities.
  I have a few messages that I need to reply to.
  I have a little time to watch TV, but not much.
- We use ***too many*** / ***too much*** to say that an amount is excessive.
  There were too many options. I didn't know what to choose!
  There was too much noise, and I couldn't sleep.
- We use ***enough*** to say that a quantity is sufficient and ***not enough*** to say that a quantity is insufficient.
  We have enough players to make two teams.
  I didn't have enough time to answer all the questions.

Should, Shouldn't, and *Ought To*

	Affirmative	Negative
I / He / She / It / We / You / They	should help.	shouldn't help.
Questions		
Should	I / he / she / it / we / you / they	help?
Short Answers		
Yes,	I / he / she / it / we / you / they	should.
No,		shouldn't.

- We use ***should*** to say what we think is a good idea or important to do – to give advice and recommendations.
  You should stay in bed if you have a fever.
  Laura shouldn't use her phone before bed.
- ***Should*** is the same in all forms. We use the infinitive after ***should***.
  John should get more sleep.
  NOT *John ~~should to get~~ more sleep.*
- We use ***ought to*** when talking about things that are desired or ideal.
  We ought to eat a lot of fruit and vegetables every day.

GRAMMAR PRACTICE UNIT 4

Quantifiers

1 Match the beginnings of the sentences with the ends.

1 Please be quiet, there's [d]
2 Too many students [ ]
3 Yoga exercises don't take [ ]
4 You'll be tired if you have [ ]
5 Do you think there's [ ]
6 Muscles get weak if you spend [ ]

a too much time, do they?
b too many late nights.
c too many hours sitting at a desk!
d too much noise in here.
e are worried about their exams.
f too much stress in your life?

2 Complete the sentences with *a little* or *a few*.

1 I do ___a few___ yoga exercises every morning at 7 a.m.
2 Jorge can give you ________ help in the gym if you need it.
3 There are ________ adjustable desks in our classroom.
4 You should do ________ exercise during long study sessions.
5 Karla needs ________ more time to finish her homework.
6 Stop working for ________ minutes and take a walk.

3 Put the words in the correct order.

1 the / time / didn't / We / to / test / have / enough / finish
We didn't have enough time to finish the test.
2 bike / enough / buy / Gisela / to / a / money / new / has
____
3 team / make / There / students / a / are / enough / to
____
4 drive / old / you / car / Are / a / enough / to / ?
____
5 me / adjustable / enough / This / high / isn't / desk / for
____

4 (Circle) the correct option.

1 (*A few*) / *A little* new students joined our swimming class.
2 I have *time enough* / *enough time* to help you.
3 These desks cost *too much* / *too many* money.
4 There were *a little* / *a few* problems we couldn't solve.
5 Does everyone have *too much* / *too many* stress in their lives?
6 Emilio does *a little* / *a few* exercise but not much.

Should, *Shouldn't*, and *Ought To*

5 Complete the sentences with *should*, *shouldn't*, or *ought*.

1 You ___shouldn't___ worry about the test – it'll be easy!
2 Melody ________ to go to bed early and get more sleep.
3 ________ Emily stay at home if she's feeling sick?
4 I ________ to eat more fish, but I don't really like it.
5 We ________ buy too many sweet things – they're bad for our teeth.

6 Underline and correct the mistake in each sentence.

1 We <u>shouldn't</u> take our coats today because it's really cold.
We should take our coats today because it's really cold.
2 Bella ought be more easygoing; she worries too much.
____
3 You should to stay in bed if you have a fever.
____
4 Who should I to ask when I need advice?
____
5 We shouldn't all drink enough water.
____

7 Complete the text with the phrases in the box.

ought to ask	ought to do	should find
should listen	~~should read~~	shouldn't start

Top tips for improving your English

You [1] ___should read___ English language magazines or websites. You [2] ________ this as often as possible. If you like reading, you [3] ________ English books or stories, but you [4] ________ your teacher for recommendations. You [5] ________ with something that's too difficult. You [6] ________ to as much English as possible too, like podcasts, radio, and TV.

The First Conditional

If- Clause	Main Clause
(*if* + simple present)	[*will*/*won't*, *may*/*might* (*not*), *could*]
If I pass all my exams,	my parents will / may / might buy me a present.
If I don't pass all my exams,	I won't / may not / might not go on vacation.
Unless I pass all my exams,	
Main Clause	***If*- Clause**
[*will*/*won't*, *may*/*might* (*not*), *could*]	(*if* + simple present)
My parents will / may / might buy me a present	if I pass my exams.
My parents won't buy me a present	if I don't pass all my exams.
	unless I pass all my exams.
Questions	
Will my parents buy me a present	if I don't pass all my exams?

- We use **first conditional** sentences to talk about possible situations in the present or future and say what we think the result will be.
- We often use ***if*** + **simple present** to describe the possible action or event.
  We'll pass the exam if we work hard.
- We can use ***unless*** + **simple present** instead of *if not*.
  Unless we hurry up, we'll miss the train.
- We use ***will***/***won't*** + **infinitive** when we are sure of the result and ***may***, ***might*** or ***could*** + **infinitive** when we are less sure.
  If we don't leave now, we won't catch the 8:30 bus.
  If my grandfather doesn't feel better, he may not visit this weekend.
  I might go the beach if it's warm enough.
  If I'm lucky, I could win the race tomorrow.
- When we use ***if*** to start the sentence, we use a comma between the two parts.
  If I have enough money, I'll go on vacation.
- We normally use ***will*** to make first conditional questions. It is unusual to use ***may*** or ***might***.
  Will you chat with me online this evening if you have time?

The Second Conditional

If- Clause	Main Clause
(*if* + simple past)	(*would*/*could*/*might* + infinitive)
If I knew him,	I would / could / might ask him.
If I didn't know him,	I wouldn't / couldn't / might not ask him.
Main Clause	***If*- Clause**
(*would*/*could*/*might* + infinitive)	(*if* + simple past)
I would / could / might ask him	if I knew him.
I wouldn't / couldn't / might not ask him	if I didn't know him.
Questions	
Would you ask him	if you knew him?

- We use the **second conditional** to talk about imaginary situations in the present and their possible consequences.
- We use ***if*** + **simple past** (affirmative or negative) to describe the imaginary situation and ***would***, ***could***, or ***might*** for the consequence.
  If he didn't like you, he wouldn't talk to you.
- We use ***would*** (***not***) when we are sure of the consequence.
  He would do better in school if he didn't spend all his time playing computer games.
- We use ***could*** (***not***) to express a possibility or ability as a consequence.
  If it was Saturday, we could go out for pizza.
  I could do some volunteer work if I didn't need to study so much.
- We use ***might*** (***not***) to show we are less sure about the consequence.
  If I had more free time, I might take up the guitar.
  Madison might lend you her laptop if you asked her.
- We can use ***was*** or ***were*** in the ***if***- part of the sentence with *I*, *he*, *she*, and *it*.
  If it wasn't/weren't so spicy, I could finish it.
  I wouldn't say anything if I were/was you.

GRAMMAR PRACTICE

The First Conditional

1 Circle the correct option.

1 If I (have) / *will have* enough time, I'll help you pick up litter.
2 Unless Jenny calls, we *don't know / won't know* where she is.
3 Many more fish will die if they *eat / will eat* our plastic waste.
4 *If / Unless* we use solar power, we will reduce air pollution.
5 We might go swimming later if the sun *comes / will come* out.

2 Put the phrases in the correct order.

1 I might / I have enough money, / If / buy a new phone
If I have enough money, I might buy a new phone.
2 come to school later / you feel better / if / Will you / ?
____
3 if / Henry will / he leaves last / turn off the lights
____
4 climate change, / our planet / Unless / we stop / will get hotter
____
5 we'll miss / we don't leave soon, / the beginning of the movie / If
____
6 we collect all the plastic / The ocean / if / might get cleaner
____

The Second Conditional

3 Circle the correct option.

1 Our planet would be in danger if all the insects *would disappear* / (*disappeared*).
2 What *would you do / did you do* if someone gave you a plastic straw?
3 Where *would you travel / would you traveled* if you had enough money?
4 There would be more oxygen if they *wouldn't destroy / didn't destroy* rainforests.
5 We could reduce the effects of climate change if we *would use / used* solar power.

4 Complete the second conditional sentences with the correct form of the words in parentheses.

1 If I had (have) the answer to the problems of climate change, I would tell (tell) you.
2 She __________ (not ask) you to come if she __________ (not like) you.
3 We __________ (not endanger) animals so much if we __________ (not destroy) their habitats.
4 If we __________ (live) near the ocean, I think our home __________ (be) in danger.
5 I __________ (not eat) meat if I __________ (be) you.

5 Underline and correct the mistake in each sentence.

1 What would you do if you <u>had won</u> a million dollars?
What would you do if you won a million dollars?
2 If you didn't work so hard, you would get so stressed.
____
3 Would those animals safer if they lived in a zoo?
____
4 I didn't eat fish unless I lived near the ocean.
____

6 Write second conditional sentences about the problems.

1 I don't have enough money to buy a new phone
have more money / buy a new phone
If I had more money, I would buy a new phone.
2 This coffee isn't sweet enough.
this coffee / be better / if / you add / a little sugar to it
____
3 We're not healthy because the air is polluted.
we all / be healthier / if / the air / not polluted
____
4 There are enough insects to feed everybody.
if / we all / eat insects / nobody / be hungry
____

Simple Present Passive

	Affirmative		Negative			
This bottle	is	made of plastic.	isn't		made of plastic.	
These toys	are		aren't			
Questions			**Short Answers**			
Is	this bottle	made of plastic?	Yes,	it is.	No,	it isn't.
Are	these toys			they are.		they aren't.

- We use the **passive** form to describe actions and processes when we are not interested in, or don't know, who is responsible for the action or process.
  English is spoken in many countries.
  Many plastic bottles aren't recycled.
- To form the **simple present passive**, we use ***is/are*** (***not***) + **past participle**.
  The streets are cleaned on Sundays after the market finishes.
- We form questions with ***Is/Are*** + **subject** + **past participle**.
  Is the main square decorated during the festival?
  When are the results sent to students?

Simple Past Passive

	Affirmative		Negative			
The trash	was	thrown away.	wasn't		thrown away.	
The old chairs	were		weren't			
Questions			**Short Answers**			
Was	the trash	thrown away?	Yes,	it was.	No,	it wasn't.
Were	the old chairs			they were.		they weren't.

- We use the **simple past passive** to describe actions and processes in the past.
  The contest winners were given books and a certificate.
- To form the **simple past passive**, we use ***was/were*** (***not***) + **past participle**.
  The first CD was made in 1982.
  Some of us weren't invited to the party.
- To form questions, we use ***was/were*** + **subject** + **past participle**.
  Were the instructions written in Spanish or Portuguese?

Passive + *By*

- We use ***by*** with the **passive** to show who or what was responsible for the action.
  The Merchant of Venice *was written by Shakespeare.*
  A lot of houses were destroyed by the fire.

Simple Present Passive

1 Complete the conversation with the simple present passive form of the verbs in parentheses.

ANA How much waste [1] _is recycled_ (recycle) in your home?

DAN Well, glass and metal [2] ______ (collect) every week. I'm not sure what [3] ______ (do) with the other materials we recycle. Some waste [4] ______ (burn).

ANA Yes, but burning waste isn't great. The air [5] ______ (pollute) because dangerous gases like methane [6] ______ (create).

DAN True, but you can do simple things to help. I never buy fruit that [7] ______ (pack) in plastic, and very little energy [8] ______ (waste) in our apartment.

2 Complete the text with the simple present passive form of the verbs in the box.

~~eat~~ fly not grow pack process produce sell send

A lot of the food that [1] _is eaten_ in the UK [2] ______ there. Oranges, for example, [3] ______ in California. They [4] ______ there and then they [5] ______ to airports in Europe. Trucks transport the fruit to towns, where they [6] ______ in supermarkets. Incredibly, some food [7] ______ by ship to China, where it [8] ______ before returning to Europe.

3 Circle the correct option to complete the sentences.

1 Where … ?
   a did BMW cars produce
   (b) are BMW cars produced
   c produced BMW cars by

2 The equipment … in a small factory near here.
   a is pack   b packed   c is packed

3 A very strong tape … these boxes.
   a is secured   b secures   c are secured

4 Their work … every day by the managers.
   a inspects   b is inspecting   c is inspected

5 The end product … for many different things.
   a uses   b is used   c has used

Simple Past Passive

4 Complete the sentences with the simple past passive form of the verbs in parentheses.

1 The Frisbee _was invented_ (invent) by American college students.

2 The Shard ______ (build) near the river in London.

3 My favorite picture ______ (paint) by Frida Kahlo.

4 The factory workers ______ (not pay) very much.

5 English ______ (speak) in many of the resorts.

5 Write questions using the simple past passive.

1 what clothes / wear / by teenagers in the 1950s
   What clothes were worn by teenagers in the 1950s?

2 who / that amazing building / design by
   ______

3 where / the American soldiers / send
   ______

4 what / those old wooden boxes / use for
   ______

6 Answer the questions in Exercise 5. Use the information given.

1 blue jeans and T-shirts
   Blue jeans and T-shirts were worn by teenagers in the 1950s.

2 Frank Lloyd Wright
   ______

3 to Europe
   ______

4 packing equipment
   ______

7 Rewrite the questions using the simple past passive with *by* in your notebooks.

1 Who found those beautiful cave paintings?
   Who were those beautiful cave paintings found by?

2 What destroyed the city of Pompeii?

3 Who wrote *Romeo and Juliet*?

4 Who built Machu Picchu?

Past Perfect

Affirmative	
I / You / He / She / It / We / You / They	had forgotten.

Negative	
I / You / He / She / It / We / You / They	hadn't (had + not) forgotten.

Questions		
Had	I / you / he / she / it / we / you / they	forgotten?

Short Answers		
Yes,	I / you / he / she / it / we / you / they	had.
No,		hadn't.

- We use the **past perfect** with other past tenses to talk about actions or states that happened before the main past action or state.
  We hadn't seen the news, so we didn't know about the storms.
  I couldn't call you on Friday because I had left my phone at home.

Reported Statements

	Direct speech	Reported Speech
Simple Present	"I **want** some new jeans."	He said (that) he **wanted** some new jeans.
Present Continuous	"We**'re making** our own clothes."	He said (that) they **were making** their own clothes.
Simple Past	"I **had** a great time."	She said (that) she**'d had** a great time.
Present Perfect	"We**'ve just seen** a live concert."	She said (that) they**'d just seen** a live concert.

- When we report somebody's words, we often have to change the verb forms – see the chart above for how the verb forms change.
- We often need to change pronouns in reported speech.
  "<u>You</u> have to arrive before 7 p.m." – He said (that) <u>we</u> had to arrive before 7 p.m.

GRAMMAR PRACTICE

UNIT 7

Past Perfect

1 Complete the sentences with the past perfect form of the verbs in parentheses.

1 I couldn't go to the performance because I *had been* (be) sick.

2 She ________ (not sleep) very well, so she felt tired all day.

3 I was happy because my team ________ (win).

4 We realized that we ________ (meet) once before.

5 He ________ (know) about the event for a long time.

2 Circle the correct option.

1 When we arrived, the party ....
  a already was started.
  b has already started.
  (c) had already started.

2 I didn't want to see the movie until I ... the book.
  a was read b had read c hadn't read

3 When we heard the noise, we knew something ....
  a had happened. b happened. c happens.

4 They were so late that the performance ....
  a has nearly finished.
  b nearly had finished.
  c had nearly finished.

5 Yolanda ran to the station, but the train ....
  a had just leave.
  b had just left.
  c was just left.

Reported Statements

3 Circle the correct option.

1 They (*say*) / *tell* that it's the biggest fair in the world.

2 Edwin *said* / *told* everyone that he wasn't coming.

3 Did anyone *say* / *tell* you what time the movie started?

4 I have already *said* / *told* you not to do that.

5 The ticket *says* / *tells* that costumes are optional.

4 Write the direct speech in reported speech.

1 "I had an interesting vacation."
He said (that) *he'd had an interesting vacation*.

2 "I've already read the movie review."
Maria said (that) ________.

3 "We're making pizzas for dinner."
They said (that) ________.

4 "Juan can't leave before eight."
I told them (that) ________.

5 Write the reported speech in direct speech.

1 She said she'd bought tickets for the exhibition.
"*I've bought tickets for the exhibition.*"

2 He told me he didn't watch any daytime TV.
"________"

3 Jacky said she was waiting for her friend to arrive.
"________"

4 We told them we had never heard that band.
"________"

6 Read the email. Then complete the reported speech below.

Home Inbox Sent **New**

Hi Diana,

Bernie and I are having an awesome time in Rio! We're staying near the Copacabana beach, so we've swum every day. The festival has been amazing. I've never seen so many fabulous costumes. We've loved every minute! Actually, we don't want to leave!

Love, Susie

I've just gotten an email from Susie, who's in Rio with Bernie. She said they [1] *were having* an awesome time. She said they [2] ________ near the Copacabana beach, so they [3] ________ every day. She wrote that the festival [4] ________ amazing. She said that she [5] ________ so many fabulous costumes. She told me that they [6] ________ every minute. Actually, they [7] ________ to leave!

To Be Allowed To

Affirmative / Negative		
I	'm / 'm not	allowed to run.
We / You / They	're / aren't	
He / She / It	's / isn't	

Questions			Short Answers
Am	I	allowed to run?	Yes, I am.
			No, I'm not.
Are	we / you / they		Yes, we / you / they are.
			No, we / you / they aren't.
Is	he / she / it		Yes, he / she / it is.
			No, he / she / it isn't.

- We use ***to be allowed to*** to say that we have permission to do something.
  We're allowed to use my aunt's laptop.
  You're not allowed to take this book out of the library.
- We often contract ***to be*** in negative sentences.
  They aren't allowed to have phones in class.
  He isn't allowed to go to the party.

Must / Must not

	Affirmative	Negative
I / He / She / It / We / You / They	must go.	must not go.

- We use ***must*** to say what we think it is necessary to do, to talk about obligation, and to give strong recommendations.
  I must start studying more.
  You must listen to this song. It's fantastic!
- We use ***must not*** to say what we think it is necessary not to do, to talk about prohibition, and to give strong advice against something.
  We must not forget to buy her a present.
  Tell them that they must not be late tomorrow.
- Questions with ***must*** are not very common as they sound very formal. We tend to use ***have to*** instead.
  Must I go to bed so early?
  Do I have to go to bed so early?
- ***Must*** is the same in all forms.
- We use an infinitive after ***must***.

To Need To

Affirmative / Negative	
I / We / You / They	need to work. / don't need to work.
He / She / It	needs to work. / doesn't need to work.

Questions		
Do	I / we / you / they	need to work?
Does	he / she / it	

Short Answers					
Yes,	I / we / you / they	do.	No,	I / we / you / they	don't.
	he / she / it	does.		he / she / it	doesn't.

- We use ***need to*** to say that there is an obligation to do something.
  I need to go home after class.
- We use ***don't need to*** to say there is no obligation to do something.
  I don't need to take the bus. I can walk.

To Have To

Affirmative / Negative	
I / We / You / They	have to learn / don't have to learn.
He / She / It	has to learn / doesn't have to learn.

Questions		
Do	I / we / you / they	have to learn?
Does	he / she / it	

Short Answers					
Yes,	I / we / you / they	do.	No,	I / we / you / they	don't.
	he / she / it	does.		he / she / it	doesn't.

- We use ***have to*** to say what it is necessary to do.
  You have to answer all the questions on the exam.
  He has to wear a uniform to school.
- We use ***don't have to*** to say that it is not necessary to do something, but that you can do it if you want.
  You don't have to help me with my homework.
  Elsie doesn't have to get up early tomorrow.
- Question words go at the beginning of the question.
  How much homework do you have to do every day?
  When do we have to make a decision?

Can/Can't, To Be Allowed To

1 Write affirmative [+] or negative [–] sentences with *can* or *can't*.

1 Susanna / come with us tomorrow. [–]
Susanna can't come with us tomorrow.
2 we / write in our English books. [+]
______
3 James / use his brother's bike. [+]
______
4 they / play in a professional orchestra. [–]
______

2 Write sentences with *to be allowed to* and the verb in parentheses.

1 We 're allowed to wear (wear) boots in the winter.
2 Andrea ______ (have) her laptop in class.
3 Franklin ______ (not / drive) his father's car.
4 Children ______ (not / be) rude to their parents.

3 Make questions and short answers with *to be allowed to*.

1 your teachers / give detention / yes
Are your teachers allowed to give detention?
Yes, they are.
2 your little sister / wear makeup / no
______
______
3 they / use online dictionaries / yes
______
______
4 we / eat all these cupcakes / no
______
______
5 Carlos / play soccer with us / yes
______
______

To Have To, Must, and To Need To

4 Underline and correct the mistake in each sentence.

1 She don't have to sit at the front of the class.
She doesn't have to sit at the front of the class.
2 You have be well-behaved on the school bus.
______
3 Luis and his friend needs to finish their homework.
______
4 Must we to come into school on the weekend?
______

5 Circle the correct option.

1 It isn't necessary to write a thank-you letter.
(a) You don't have to write a letter.
b You must not write a letter.
2 I can go to the gym by bike.
a I need to take the bus.
b I don't need to take the bus.
3 It's important for me to study for exams.
a I don't need to study. b I must study.
4 We're not allowed to run in the hallways.
a We don't have to run, but we can.
b We must not run.
5 You must watch this video!
a I strongly recommend it.
b I don't think you'll like it.

6 Complete the swimming pool rules with the phrases in the box.

don't have to use don't need to bring have to have have to wear must remember ~~must not come~~ must not run need to pay

You [1] must not come into the pool area in outdoor shoes. You [2] ______ rubber shoes around the pool. You [3] ______ attention on wet surfaces, and you [4] ______ at any time. There are lockers in the changing rooms, but you [5] ______ them. You [6] ______ your own towel because towels are provided. However, if you do use ours, you [7] ______ to leave them in the basket provided. Finally, swimmers under the age of ten [8] ______ an accompanying adult.

To Be Going To

Affirmative / Negative			Questions	
I	'm / 'm not	going to tell him.	Am I	going to tell him?
He / She / It	's / isn't		Is he / she / it	
We / You / They	're / aren't		Are we / you / they	

Short Answers			
Yes,	I am.	No,	I'm not.
	he / she / it is.		he / she / it isn't.
	we / you / they are.		we / you / they aren't.

- We use ***to be going to*** to talk about future actions we have decided to do.
  After we finish school, I'm going to travel to Australia.
  My grandparents are going to stay with us this summer.
- We use the appropriate present form of ***to be*** (***not***) + ***going*** + ***to*** + **verb**.
  I'm going to wear my new jeans and my red T-shirt.
  We're not going to take the bus.
- We form questions with ***to be*** + **subject** + ***going*** + ***to*** + **verb**.
  When are you going to start studying for the exams?
  Is she going to get here before nine o'clock?

Present Continuous for Future

- We use the **present continuous** to talk about future arrangements when they have a fixed date.
  They're getting married this summer.
  What are you doing this weekend? I'm going shopping with my parents.

Future Continuous

Affirmative / Negative		
I / You / He / She / It / We / You / They	will / won't	be lying on the beach this time next week.
	may / may not	
	might / might not	

Questions			Short Answers
Will	I / you / he / she / it / we / you / they	be lying on the beach this time next week?	Yes, I / you / he / she / it / we / you / they will.
			No, I / you / he / she / it / we / you / they won't.

- We can use the **future continuous** to talk about actions in progress at a point in time in the future.
  My sister will be living in Mexico next year.
  Next Saturday, we'll be sitting on the beach.
- We use ***will***/***won't*** when we feel sure about the action in progress, and ***may*** (***not***) / ***might*** (***not***) when we're less sure.
  They'll be answering questions online at 7 p.m.
  We might be having dinner at 9 p.m.

Relative Pronouns and Relative Clauses

- We use **relative clauses** to make the person, place, or thing we are talking about clear.
  My aunt has a friend who makes beautiful bags.
  This is the song that I told you about.
- We use **relative pronouns** at the beginning of relative clauses. We do not repeat the subject pronoun when the subject of the pronoun and following clause are the same.
  We know a lot of people who live in the village.
  NOT ~~We know a lot of people who they live in the village.~~
- We use ***who*** or ***that*** to talk about people.
  The man who/that lives next door works at night.
  She's the scientist who's/that's moving to Antarctica next year.
- We use ***that*** to talk about things.
  I don't like books that have sad endings.
  I want boots that I can wear all year.
- We use ***where*** to talk about places.
  That's the office where my uncle works.
  Try the restaurant where we had my party.
- We use ***when*** to talk about time.
  That was the day when we were late for school.
  It's the holiday when everyone is happiest.
- We use ***why*** to talk about reasons.
  You studied a lot. That's the reason why you passed!
  I lost my passport. That's the reason why I'm so sad.
- We use ***whose*** to talk about possessions.
  Do you remember the name of the guy whose phone charger I borrowed last week?

GRAMMAR PRACTICE

UNIT 9

To Be Going To

1 Complete the sentences with the correct form of *to be going to* and the verb in parentheses.

1 We ___are going to visit___ (visit) our old neighbors on the weekend.

2 She ____________ (not come) with us to Peru.

3 He ____________ (leave) for the station at nine.

4 They ____________ (deliver) the products by drone next year.

5 Flights ____________ (not be) cheaper in future, are they?

6 ____________ you ____________ (buy) the train tickets online?

Present Continuous for Future

2 Put the words in the correct order.

1 train / traveling / on / to / the / night / Madrid / We're

___We're traveling to Madrid on the night train.___

2 meeting / the / friends / their / They're / on / bus

____

3 on / summer / going / I'm / trip / this / school / a

____

4 for / you / Are / birthday / having / a / your / party / ?

____

5 tonight / isn't / our / Stella / to / concert / coming

____

Future Continuous

3 Complete the text with the phrases in the box.

will be building	will be cycling	~~will be driving~~
will be making	will be using	won't be doing

More people [1] ___will be driving___ electric cars in the future. Transportation companies [2] ____________ driverless trucks, too. But I wonder how teenagers [3] ____________ their daily trips in 20 years? Many believe that they [4] ____________ more, but they [5] ____________ that unless road conditions are improved. Today's cyclists hope that town planners [6] ____________ more bike lanes by the time their children are teenagers.

Relative Pronouns and Relative Clauses

4 (Circle) the correct option.

1 I didn't know the person (who) / *whose* sat next to me.

2 She's the girl *who* / *whose* mother is from Chile.

3 Is August the time *which* / *when* it rains a lot in Scotland?

4 This is the book *that* / *whose* was banned in the 1940s.

5 That's the place *why* / *where* they used to meet.

6 It's the summer and that's *where* / *why* I'm happy!

5 Underline and correct the mistake in each sentence.

1 Do you know <u>who</u> bags these are?

___Do you know whose bags these are?___

2 She can't remember when she wanted to buy.

____

3 That is the language school she will be studying.

____

4 I'll never forget the time why I met Adele.

____

5 Is there a reason where you don't want to fly?

____

6 Complete the conversation with the phrases in the box and the correct relative pronoun: *where*, *why*, *that*, *whose*, or *who*.

father was the artist	she recommended	told us
was the artist	we could wait	~~you took~~

ALEXIA Are those the photos [1] ___that you took___ on vacation?

KARL Yes, I took this one in Paris, remember?

ALEXIA Oh, I remember! We found a museum [2] ____________ for the rain to stop.

KARL That's right! This was the girl [3] ____________ about the exhibition.

ALEXIA I don't remember her. Was she the person [4] ____________?

KARL No, it wasn't her father, but she knew the man [5] ____________. That's the reason [6] ____________ the exhibition.

STARTER

Vocabulary

Technology

app device emoji screen
social media video chat

Feelings

angry bored embarrassed
excited nervous upset

Music

bass guitar country DJ drums fans
heavy metal jazz keyboard rap reggae

Grammar in Action

Simple Present and Present Continuous with Adverbs of Frequency
Simple Present and Present Continuous for Future
Simple Past

Writing

Useful Language

Writing a Review of an App

… is a(n) … app
It's great because …
In my opinion, there are a couple of problems with it.
Overall, I think it's …
I really recommend it.

UNIT 1

Vocabulary

Describing People

active ambitious calm cheerful
confident helpful inspiring patient
sensible sensitive sociable talented

Phrasal Verbs

cheer (somebody) up
deal with
depend on
get along with
give up
hang out
look up to
take care of

Grammar in Action

Simple Past and Past Continuous with *When* and *While*
Used To

Speaking

Everyday English

Go ahead.
Good for (her)!
I'm with you there.
The thing is …

Useful Language

Can I ask you a few questions … ?
Can you tell us … ?
First of all, …
One more thing …
That's all …

Writing

Useful Language

Writing a Letter to a Magazine

For me, …
In my opinion, …
In my view, …
Personally, I think …

LANGUAGE BANK

UNIT 2

Vocabulary

Visual and Performing Arts

architecture contemporary dance exhibition fashion design filmmaking gallery illustration musical theater performance photography sculpture street art

Music and Theater

audience audition lines lyrics orchestra part rehearsal scene show studio

Grammar in Action

Present perfect with regular and irregular verbs
Present perfect with *already*, *just*, *still*, and *yet*

Speaking

Everyday English

dunno
ginormous
kid
nope
tons

Useful Language

It isn't supposed to …
It looks like …
It makes me feel …
It probably shows …
It seems a little …

Writing

Useful Language

Writing a Review

I recommend it because …
It's playing at …
It's the best show I've ever seen.
I've never seen anything like it before.
What I liked / didn't like about it was …

UNIT 3

Vocabulary

Communicating

describe gesture greet interpret post shake hands shout smile translate wave whisper

Collocations with *To Say* and *To Tell*

Say: hello / something in Italian / sorry / yes/no
Tell: a joke / a lie / a story / someone a secret / the truth

Grammar in Action

Can, Could, Will Be Able To
Present Perfect with *How long* … ? and *For/Since*
Present Perfect and Simple Past

Speaking

Everyday English

Oh, no!
Phew!
Sure thing.
Yep.

Useful Language

I need them to …
It's a kind of …
They're similar to …
You use it to …

Writing

Useful Language

Writing a Listicle

all (his) life
before
later on
over the last few years
since
soon
these days

LANGUAGE BANK

UNIT 4

Vocabulary

Health and Fitness

cough | get better | get enough sleep | get sick | get stressed | go jogging | have a fever | relax | sneeze | sweat | train | warm up | work out

Healthy Eating

a balanced diet | calories | carbohydrates | dairy products | fat | fiber | nutrition | protein | vitamins

Grammar in Action

Quantifiers
Should, *Shouldn't*, and *Ought To*

Speaking

Everyday English

I'll give it a try.
… isn't really my thing.
Seriously?
Tell me about it!

Useful Language

How about … (+ *-ing*)?
Make sure you …
Something else I find useful …
… works for me.
You could just …

Writing

Useful Language

Writing a Post on a Forum

Have you tried … (+ *-ing*)?
I recommend … (+ *-ing*)
That way, you can just …
Why don't you … ?
You could always …

UNIT 5

Vocabulary

Planet Earth

carbon dioxide | climate change | endangered species | energy | marine life | oxygen | pollution | solar power | the environment | the planet | waste | wildlife

Natural Environments

bay | cave | cliff | coast | iceberg | rainforest | stream | valley | volcano | waterfall

Grammar in Action

The First Conditional
The Second Conditional

Speaking

Everyday English

I'll have to pass.
I'm off to …
It's not cool.
Wanna join us?

Useful Language

Don't forget that …
I see your point, but …
Let's agree to disagree.
Maybe you're right, but …
Remember that …

Writing

Useful Language

Writing an Opinion Essay

Furthermore, …
However, …
In addition, …
In my opinion, …
In my view, …
In summary, …
Some people believe that …

LANGUAGE BANK

UNIT 6

Vocabulary

Making Things

add boil cover dip freeze
increase place pour press pull
reduce remove stir

Materials

cardboard glass
leather rubber silk tin

Containers

bag box can
case jar tube

Grammar in Action

Simple Present Passive
Simple Past Passive

Speaking

Everyday English

any old …
Go for it!
Hang on a sec!
I get it.
kind of tricky

Useful Language

Giving Instructions

And there you have it!
First of all, …
Once (something is done), …
The next part's …

Following Instructions

Let me get this straight.
Oh, I see.
Then what?
What's next?

Writing

Useful Language

Writing a Review

The glasses look like …
The lenses are made from …
What I like about them is …
However, I should point out that …
Overall, I think it is / they are …

UNIT 7

Vocabulary

Festivals

atmosphere ceremony costume
crowd decoration fair fireworks float
lantern parade program stall

Music Festivals and Live Music

band member campsite encore
gig headliner stage supporting act
tent track venue

Grammar in Action

Past Perfect
Reported Statements

Speaking

Everyday English

at my place
Count me in.
It kicks off at …
I won't say a word.
The more the merrier.

Useful Language

I'd love to.
I'll be there (at/around) …
Should I bring anything?
What are you up to … ?
What time should I be there?

Writing

Useful Language

Writing an Email to a Friend

Anyway, that's all from me.
Bye for now,
It was great to hear from you!
Thanks for your email.
Write back soon!

UNIT 8

Vocabulary

School

cheat on a test fail an exam get detention get good grades give (somebody) a talk hand in homework pass an exam pay attention to the teacher study for a test take an exam write an essay

Attitude and Behavior

careful careless disobedient disorganized immature mature organized polite rude well-behaved

Grammar in Action

Can/Can't
To Be Allowed To
To Have To, *Must*, and *To Need To*

Speaking

Everyday English

How come?
Kind of.
That's no big deal.
Yeah, right!

Useful Language

Anything else I need to know?
What are the rules about … ?
What happens if you do?
Why's that?

Writing

Useful Language

Writing an Essay

In this essay, I outline …
On the one hand, …
On the other hand, …
Others argue that …
Some say that …

UNIT 9

Vocabulary

Travel

abroad accommodation backpacking book cruise ship destination journey resort sightseeing tour tourist attraction trip

Travel Phrasal Verbs

check in check out get away get back get in go away look around set off take off

Grammar in Action

To Be Going To and Present Continuous for Future
Future Continuous
Relative Pronouns and Relative Clauses

Speaking

Everyday English

… and so on.
bucket list
… right in the middle of …
the usual stuff
What were you saying?

Useful Language

How long are you going for?
I'm really looking forward to … (+ *-ing*)
… in two weeks
We're going to try …
What are you planning on doing?
Where will you be staying?

Writing

Useful Language

Writing an Email to a Host Family

Best wishes,
Dear Mr. and Mrs. …
Do you know … ?
I'm writing to …
Thank you very much for (+ *-ing*)

IRREGULAR VERBS

Infinitive	Simple Past	Past Participle
be	was/were	been
beat	beat	beaten
become	became	become
begin	began	begun
bite	bit	bitten
blow	blew	blown
break	broke	broken
bring	brought	brought
build	built	built
buy	bought	bought
catch	caught	caught
choose	chose	chosen
come	came	come
cost	cost	cost
cut	cut	cut
do	did	done
draw	drew	drawn
drink	drank	drunk
drive	drove	driven
eat	ate	eaten
fall	fell	fallen
feel	felt	felt
fight	fought	fought
find	found	found
fly	flew	flown
forget	forgot	forgotten
get	got	gotten
give	gave	given
go	went	gone
grow	grew	grown
hang	hung	hung
have	had	had
hear	heard	heard
hide	hid	hidden
hit	hit	hit
hold	held	held
hurt	hurt	hurt
keep	kept	kept
know	knew	known
leave	left	left
lend	lent	lent

Infinitive	Simple Past	Past Participle
let	let	let
lie	lied	lied
light	lit	lit
lose	lost	lost
make	made	made
mean	meant	meant
meet	met	met
pay	paid	paid
put	put	put
read	read	read
ride	rode	ridden
ring	rang	rung
rise	rose	risen
run	ran	run
say	said	said
see	saw	seen
sell	sold	sold
send	sent	sent
shine	shone	shone
shoot	shot	shot
show	showed	shown
shut	shut	shut
sing	sang	sung
sit	sat	sat
sleep	slept	slept
speak	spoke	spoken
spend	spent	spent
stand	stood	stood
steal	stole	stolen
swim	swam	swum
take	took	taken
teach	taught	taught
tear	tore	torn
tell	told	told
think	thought	thought
throw	threw	thrown
understand	understood	understood
wake	woke	woken
wear	wore	worn
win	won	won
write	wrote	written

ACKNOWLEDGEMENTS

The authors and publishers acknowledge the following sources of copyright material and are grateful for the permissions granted. While every effort has been made, it has not always been possible to identify the sources of all the material used, or to trace all copyright holders. If any omissions are brought to our notice, we will be happy to include the appropriate acknowledgements on reprinting & in the next update to the digital edition, as applicable.

Key: **SU** = Starter Unit, **U** = Unit

Text

U1: Text about Derek Rabelo. Copyright © Derek Rabelo. Reproduce with permission; **U2:** Text about Lorenzo Quinn. Copyright © Lorenzo Quinn. Reproduced with kind permission; Text about Alma Deutscher. Copyright © Alma Deutscher. Reproduced with kind permission of Guy Deutscher.

Photography

The following photographs are sourced from Getty Images.

SU: Monkey Business Images/Getty Images Plus; Viktor Holm/Folio; Sidekick/E+; Pekic/E+; Mima Foto/EyeEm; **U1:** PT Images; Westend61; GRANT ELLIS/AFP; Ryan McVay/Photodisc; Ulrik Tofte/Photodisc; Jupiterimages/Stockbyte; Morsa Images/DigitalVision; Compassionate Eye Foundation/Jetta Productions/Stockbyte; Lawrence Manning/Corbis; Klisarova/Moment; Klaus Vedfelt/DigitalVision; fizkes/iStock/Getty Images Plus; Digital Vision; **U2:** David_Ahn/iStock/Getty Images Plus; Hill Street Studios/DigitalVision; Daria Botieva/Eyeem; ollo/iStock Unreleased; Kathrin Ziegler/DigitalVision; starman72/RooM; Zero Creatives/Cultura; kpalimski/iStock/Getty Images Plus; Brian Caissie; Adam Berry/Getty Images News; JOE KLAMAR/AFP; Mike Harrington/DigitalVision; Hero Images; fStop Images-Holger Hill/Brand X Pictures; Foodcollection RF; Ryan McVay/Photodisc; Ariel Skelley/DigitalVision; miodrag ignjatovic/E+; Fuse/Corbis; **U3:** MikeCherim/E+; Westend61; praetorianphoto/E+; Tetra Images; Juanmonino/iStock/Getty Images Plus; Blend Images-KidStock/Brand X Pictures; Rene Frederick/Photodisc; Juanmonino/iStock/Getty Images Plus; recep-bg/E+; hkuchera/iStock/Getty Images Plus; Erik Isakson/Blend Images; Jose Luis Pelaez Inc/Blend Images; **U4:** Stanislaw Pytel/DigitalVision; SCIEPRO/Science Photo Library; Jose Luis Pelaez Inc/DigitalVision; gbh007/iStock/Getty Images Plus; SolStock/E+; Hero Images; Cavan Images; Hill Street Studios/Blend Images; pixelpot/iStock/Getty Images Plus; Lemanieh/iStock/Getty Images Plus; margouillatphotos/iStock/Getty Images Plus; Ross Woodhall/Cultura; monticellllo/iStock/Getty Images Plus; filmfoto/iStock/Getty Images Plus; RascalRJ/Moment Open; apixel/E+; GMint/iStock/Getty Images Plus; Tetra Images; anouchka/iStock/Getty Images Plus; Vasily Pindyurin; Image Source; Muriel de Seze/DigitalVision; asiseeit/E+; mihailomilovanovic/E+; **U5:** Steve Clancy Photography/Moment; Peter Dazeley/Photographer's Choice RF; FotoDuets/iStock/Getty Images Plus; Gary Conner/Photodisc; Herianus Herianus/EyeEm; pepifoto/E+; Westend61; paul mansfield photography/Moment; Sebastián Crespo Photography/Moment; Photos by R A Kearton/Moment Open; Timothy Mbugua/EyeEm; zhuzhu/iStock/Getty Images Plus; JLR/Moment; Ippei Naoi/Moment; Milton Cogheil/EyeEm; Yevgen Timashov/Cultura; Paola Moschitto-Assenmacher/EyeEm; Matteo Colombo/Moment; Marko Konig; Ricardo Funari/Brazil Photos/LightRocket; Matt Cardy/Getty Images News; GREG BAKER/AFP; SeaTops; **U6:** Food Delight/EyeEm; JoKMedia/E+; Monty Rakusen/Cultura; Photographer is my life./Moment; stevanovicigor/iStock/Getty Images Plus; Kiran Ridley/Barcroft Images/Barcroft Media; hocus-focus/iStock Unreleased; Poh Kim Yeoh/EyeEm; flyfloor/E+; **U7:** Keren Su/China Span; John W Banagan/Photographer's Choice; FernandoQuevedo/iStock Editorial/Getty Images Plus; merc67/iStock Editorial/Getty Images Plus; Alexander W Helin/Moment; ©Philippe LEJEANVRE/Moment; Oscar G Davila/EyeEm; Andreas Rentz/Getty Images Entertainment; Hendra Su/EyeEm; Satoshi-K/iStock Unreleased; nevereverro/iStock Unreleased; gavran333/iStock/Getty Images Plus; 101cats/E+; Bettmann; Matthew Eisman/Redferns; Hero Images; Aleksandr_Vorobev/iStock Editorial/Getty Images Plus; olmozott98/iStock Editorial/Getty Images Plus; BILL WECHTER/AFP Contributor; Kevin Winter/Getty Images Entertainment; SAKhanPhotography/iStock/Getty Images Plus; **U8:** Digital Vision/Photodisc; Lafforgue/Art In All Of Us/Corbis News; Hero Images; piola666/E+; Wavebreakmedia/iStock/Getty Images Plus; Radius Images/Getty Images Plus; skynesher/E+; **U9:** Marka/Universal Images Group; arturbo/iStock/Getty Images Plus; iLexx/iStock/Getty Images Plus; PhonlamaiPhoto/iStock/Getty Images Plus; inhauscreative/E+; Ed Freeman/The Image Bank/Getty Images Plus; Peter Samuels/DigitalVision; AngiePhotos/E+; balipadma/iStock/Getty Images Plus.

The following photographs are sourced from other sources.

U1: Copyright © Derek Rabelo; **U2:** Courtesy of the artist Lorenzo Quinn.

Illustration

U3: Amber Day; **U4:** Joanna Kerr; **U7:** Oliver Flores; **U9:** Joanna Kerr.

Typesetting: Aphik, S.A. de C.V.

Cover design and illustrations: Collaborate Agency

Audio Recordings: Eastern Sky Studios

American English Consultant: Mandie Drucker

Freelance Editors: Sue Costello, Jacqueline French, Suzanne Harris, and Penny Nicholson